A Listening/ Speaking Skills Book

interactions one

A Listening/ Speaking Skills Book

Third Edition

interactions one

Judith Tanka
University of California, Los Angeles

Paul Most

The McGraw-Hill Companies, Inc.

New York St. Louis San Francisco Auckland Bogotá Caracas Lisbon
London Madrid Mexico City Milan Montreal New Delhi San Juan
Singapore Sydney Tokyo Toronto

This is an EDI book.

McGraw-Hill

A Division of The **McGraw·Hill** *Companies*

Interactions One
A Listening/Speaking Skills Book
Third Edition

3 4 5 6 7 8 9 0   DOC DOC   9 0 9 8 7 6

ISBN 0-07-063148-4
ISBN 0-07-114372-6

This book was set in Times Roman by Monotype Composition Company, Inc.

The editors were Tim Stookesberry, Bill Preston, and John Chapman, the designers were Lorna Lo, Suzanne Montazer, Francis Owens, and Elizabeth Williamson; the production supervisor was Patricia Myers; the cover was designed by Francis Owens; the cover illustrator was Susan Pizzo; the photo researcher was Cindy Robinson, Seaside Publishing; illustrations were done by David Bohn, Axelle Fortier, Rick Hackney, Lori Heckelman, and Sally Richardson.

R. R. Donnelley & Sons Company, Crawfordsville, IN, was printer and binder.
Phoenix Color Corporation was cover separator and printer.

Library of Congress Catalog Card Number: 95-80830

Photo credits: *Page 1* © Beryl Goldberg; *6* © Frank Tapia; *13* © David Woo/Stock, Boston; *18* © Alan Carey/Photo Researchers, Inc.; *23* © Stephen Dunn/Allsport; *25* © Jack Stein Grove/PhotoEdit; *29* © Stuart Cohen; *30* © Walter Gilardetti; *31* © Beryl Goldberg; *34 (left, center)* © Walter Gilardetti; *(right)* © Tom McCarthy/PhotoEdit; *35* © Comstock; *37* © Peter Vandermark/Stock, Boston; *42* © Donald Dietz/Stock, Boston; *47* all © Walter Gilardetti; *57* © Tony Freeman/PhotoEdit; *60* © Beryl Goldberg; *69* © Walter Gilardetti; *79* © Robert Brenner/PhotoEdit; *85* © Everett Collection; *87* © Dion Ogust/The Image Works; *97* © M. Siluk/The Image Works; *105* © P. Gontier/The Image Works; *108* © Joseph Nettis/Stock, Boston; *113* © Walter Gilardetti; *117* © Mark Richards/PhotoEdit

Contents

CHAPTER **one**
School Life

CHAPTER **two**
Experiencing Nature

CHAPTER **three**
Living to Eat or Eating to Live?

CHAPTER **four**
Getting Around the Community

CHAPTER **five**
Home

CHAPTER **six**
Emergencies and Strange Experiences

CHAPTER **seven**
Health

Preface
to the Third Edition

The Interactions One Program

The Interactions One program consists of five texts and a variety of supplemental materials for high-beginning to low-intermediate students seeking to improve their English language skills. Each of the five texts in this program is carefully organized by chapter theme, vocabulary, grammar structures, and, where possible, language functions. As a result, information introduced in a chapter of any one of the Interactions One texts corresponds to and reinforces material taught in the same chapter of the other four books, creating a truly integrated, four-skills approach.

The Interactions One program is highly flexible. The texts in this series may be used together or separately, depending on students' needs and course goals. The books in this program include:

- **A Communicative Grammar.** Organized around grammatical topics, this book includes notational/functional material where appropriate. It presents all grammar in context and contains many types of communicative activities.
- **A Listening / Speaking Skills Book.** This book uses lively, natural language from various contexts, including dialogues, interviews, lectures, and announcements. Listening strategies emphasized include summarizing main ideas, making inferences, listening for stressed words, reductions, and intonation. A variety of speaking activities complement the listening component.
- **A Reading Skills Book.** The reading selections contain sophisticated college-level material; however, vocabulary and grammar have been carefully controlled to be at students' level of comprehension. The text includes many vocabulary-building exercises and emphasizes reading strategies such as skimming, scanning, guessing meaning from context, understanding the structure and organization of a selection, increasing reading speed, and interpreting the author's point of view.
- **A Writing Process Book.** This book uses a process approach to writing, including many exercises on prewriting and revision. Exercises build skills in exploring and organizing ideas; developing vocabulary; using correct form and mechanics; using coherent structure; and editing, revising, and using feedback to create a final draft.
- **A Multi-Skills Activity Book.** New to this edition, this text gives integrated practice in all four language skills. Among the communicative activities included in this text are exercises for the new video program that accompanies the Interactions One series.

Supplemental Materials

In addition to the five core texts outlined above, various supplemental materials are available to assist users of the third edition, including:

Instructor's Manual

Extensively revised for the new edition, this manual provides instructions and guidelines for using the five core texts separately or in various combinations to suit particular program needs. For each of the core texts, there is a separate section with teaching tips, additional activities, and other suggestions. The testing materials have been greatly expanded in this edition.

Audio Program for Interactions One: A Listening/Speaking Skills Book

Completely rerecorded for the new edition, the audio program is designed to be used in conjunction with those exercises that are indicated with a cassette icon in the student text. Complete tapescripts for all exercises are now included in the back of the student text.

Audio Program to Accompany Interactions One: A Reading Skills Book

This new optional audio program contains selected readings from the student text. These tape selections of poems, articles, stories, and speeches enable students to listen at their leisure to the natural discourse of native readers for imitation and modeling. Readings that are included in this program are indicated with a cassette icon in the student text.

Video

New to this edition, the video program for Interactions One contains authentic television segments that are coordinated with the twelve chapter themes in the five texts. Exercises and activities for this video are in the Multi-Skills Activities Book.

Interactions One: A Listening/ Speaking Skills Book, Third Edition

When listening to English, lower-level students have two basic needs:

1. To understand the essence of messages beyond their level—i.e., day-to-day comprehension for survival.

2. To learn effective listening strategies that, in turn, will lead to language acquistion itself.

The traditional emphasis in typical lower-level listening texts has been on testing listening comprehension. In *Interactions One: A Listening/ Speaking Skills Book,* third edition, the emphasis is on teaching high-beginning to low-intermediate students how to develop listening comprehension through a variety of listening skills, including predicting, drawing inferences, summarizing, and identifying phonological clues that signal important information. Students apply these skills to a great variety of recorded English, such as conversation, announcements, phone messages, and radio news broadcasts. Each chapter includes both life skills and academically oriented topics, using both formal and informal language. Ongoing characters and storyline provide continuity and interest.

Chapter Organization

Each chapter contains listening skills, listening tasks, and speaking activities, divided into five parts as follows:

- **Part One—Getting the Main Idea: Stressed Words and Reduction.** As students listen to an introductory conversation, they actively focus on the stressed words that signal important information; students learn to recognize and reproduce reduced forms common in spoken American English.

- **Part Two—Summarizing Main Ideas.** Students identify and pick out relevant details from a short corpus of information, for example, conversations, department store announcements, and radio news reports. Then, based on their notes, students reconstruct the message(s) either orally or in writing.

- **Part Three—Guessing Information.** Students use contextual clues to understand implied messages in one or more conversations. In many cases, answers to questions posed in the exercise appear later in the conversation(s), so students get the benefit of immediate feedback. Because guessing information is a skill that can help students do well on standardized listening tests such as the TOEFL, this part of the chapter is now highlighted as a special feature called **Focus on Testing.**

- **Part Four—Listening Tasks.** In this section students demonstrate their comprehension by performing practical tasks involving real-life material such as drawings, maps, and application forms.

- **Part Five—Speaking Activities.** Role-plays, small-group activities, and class discussions complement the listening component. These speaking activities are natural extensions of the chapter theme and offer students imaginative opportunities to further explore it.

Teaching Suggestions

Students often assume that repeated listening to a speech sample alone will lead to comprehension. In the students' complex listening environment, that is, the real world, this type of listening is hardly practical and is usually impossible. The philosophy behind this book is that efficient listening is better achieved through selective listening, via the application of particular listening skills. Therefore, we recommend that teachers spend sufficient time in Chapter One explaining each listening skill that will be practiced repeatedly throughout the book, namely, getting the main idea, identifying stressed words and reductions, summarizing main ideas, and guessing information from context. As students become more familiar with the concept of selective listening and learn to apply listening strategies more efficiently, they will develop confidence in their ability and thus will require less teacher guidance.

Because the aim of this book is to develop (not merely test) listening comprehension, students will encounter some language that is slightly beyond their level of comprehension. Exercises and activities may seem challenging,

and it is essential that students understand clearly the instructions and goals. Therefore, we recommend that teachers spend sufficient time clarifying the purpose and method of each exercise and activity prior to assigning it.

To take advantage of the ongoing story line and graded levels of difficulty for grammar and vocabulary, it is best (but not essential) to present the chapters in order. Teachers with a structure-based curriculum can refer to the *Instructor's Manual* for a chapter-by-chapter breakdown of grammar points.

New to the Third Edition

1. **New Chapter Theme on Science and Technology.** The new edition features an entirely new theme for Chapter Eleven: Science and Technology. In addition, the themes for several other chapters have been broadened to include new content.

2. **Did you know?** These new boxed features present surprising or interesting facts to stimulate discussion of the chapter themes.

3. **Focus on Testing.** These new boxed features in every chapter are designed to help students prepare for standardized listening tests such as the TOEFL.

4. **Tapescripts.** Tapescripts for all listening exercises and activities have been included in the back of the student text.

5. **Streamlined Design.** The new edition features an attractive two-color design and an extensively revised art program. These changes were initiated to make the books more appealing, up-to-date, and user friendly. In addition, we made the books easier to use by simplifying complicated direction lines, numbering exercises and activities, and highlighting key information in shaded boxes and charts.

6. **Skill Charts.** Charts summarizing the listening skills, listening tasks, and speaking activities for all twelve chapters have been added to the preface.

Recommendations for Testing

Listening comprehension is not a skill that can be improved through the memorization of rules or discrete items. For this reason, progress in listening comprehension is not easy to test. Generally, we do not recommend giving students grades in listening because it is not something they can take home and study. However, if the teacher must give grades and tests, we recommend using the midterm and final exam which appear in the Instructor's Manual.

Acknowledgments

Our thanks to the following reviewers whose comments, both favorable and critical, were of great value in the development of the third edition of the Interactions/Mosaic series:

Jean Al-Sibai, University of North Carolina; Janet Alexander, Waterbury College; Roberta Alexander, San Diego City College; Julie Alpert, Santa Barbara City College; Anita Cook, Tidewater Community College; Anne Deal Beavers, Heald Business College; Larry Berking, Monroe Community College; Deborah Busch, Delaware County Community College; Patricia A. Card, Chaminade University of Honolulu; Jose A. Carmona, Hudson County Community College; Kathleen Carroll, Fontbonne College; Conseula Chase, Loyola University; Lee Chen, California State University; Karen Cheng, University of Malaya; Gaye Childress, University of North Texas; Maria Conforti, University of Colorado; Earsie A. de Feliz, Arkansas State University; Elizabeth Devlin-Foltz, Montgomery County Adult Education; Colleen Dick, San Francisco Institute of English; Marta Dmytrenko-Ahrabian, Wayne State University; Margo Duffy, Northeast Wisconsin Technical; Magali Duignan, Augusta College; Janet Dyar, Meridian Community College; Anne Ediger, San Diego City College; D. Frangie, Wayne State University; Robert Geryk, Wayne State University; Jeanne Gibson, American Language Academy; Kathleen Walsh Greene, Rhode Island College; Myra Harada, San Diego Mesa College; Kristin Hathhorn, Eastern Washington University; Mary Herbert, University of California–Davis; Joyce Homick, Houston Community College; Catherine Hutcheson, Texas Christian University; Suzie Johnston, Tyler Junior College; Donna Kauffman, Radford University; Emmie Lim, Cypress College; Patricia Mascarenas, Monte Vista Community School; Mark Mattison, Donnelly College; Diane Peak, Choate Rosemary Hall; James Pedersen, Irvine Valley College; Linda Quillan, Arkansas State University; Marnie Ramker, University of Illinois; Joan Roberts, The Doane Stuart School; Doralee Robertson, Jacksonville University; Ellen Rosen, Fullerton College; Jean Sawyer, American Language Academy; Frances Schulze, College of San Mateo; Sherrie R. Sellers, Brigham Young University; Tess M. Shafer, Edmonds Community College; Heinz F. Tengler, Lado International College; Sara Tipton, Wayne State University; Karen R. Vallejo, Brigham Young University; Susan Williams, University of Central Florida; Mary Shepard Wong, El Camino College; Cindy Yoder, Eastern Mennonite College; Cheryl L. Youtsey, Loyola University; Miriam Zahler, Wayne State University; Maria Zien, English Center, Miami; Yongmin Zhu, Los Medanos College; Norma Zorilla, Fresno Pacific College.

Donnelly College; Diane Peak, Choate Rosemary Hall; James Pedersen, Irvine Valley College; Linda Quillan, Arkansas State University; Marnie Ramker, University of Illinois; Joan Roberts, The Doane Stuart School; Doralee Robertson, Jacksonville University; Ellen Rosen, Fullerton College; Jean Sawyer, American Language Academy; Frances Schulze, College of San Mateo; Sherrie R. Sellers, Brigham Young University; Tess M. Shafer, Edmonds Community College; Heinz F. Tengler, Lado International College; Sara Tipton, Wayne State University; Karen R. Vallejo, Brigham Young University; Susan Williams, University of Central Florida; Mary Shepard Wong, El Camino College; Cindy Yoder, Eastern Mennonite College; Cheryl L. Youtsey, Loyola University; Miriam Zahler, Wayne State University; Maria Zien, English Center, Miami; Yongmin Zhu, Los Medanos College; Norma Zorilla, Fresno Pacific College.

Summary of Listening/Speaking Skills and Activities

Chapter	Listening Skills	Listening Tasks	Speaking Activities
one	• getting the main ideas • identifying stressed words and reductions • distinguishing -s endings • guessing information from context	• taking telephone messages from an answering machine • filling out a permit application	• summarizing key points of a speech • making introductions • talking about body language • role playing a chance encounter
two	• getting the main idea • identifying stressed words and reductions • distinguishing between *can* and *can't* • guessing information from context	• taking notes on weather forecasts and conversations about the weather	• summarizing key point of a story • describing seasons/ seasonal activities • discussing sports • talking about recycling • role playing a camping scene
three	• getting the main idea • identifying stressed words and reductions • distinguishing between *teens* and *tens* • guessing information from context	• following recipe directions • filling in a map	• summarizing advice about dieting • comparing eating habits • planning a barbecue • describing recipes • role playing a super-market scene
four	• getting the main idea • identifying stressed words and reductions • guessing information from context	• following map directions • taking notes on bus routes and schedules	• comparing big cities/ small towns • asking for/giving directions • describing a neighborhood • comparing types of transportation • role playing getting a parking citation
five	• getting the main idea • identifying stressed words and reductions • distinguishing -ed endings • guessing information from context	• filling out a change of address form • identifying places and furnishings in a house	• describing changes in a neighborhood • describing the move to a new house • role playing renting an apartment • role playing finding a roommate

Chapter	Listening Skills	Listening Tasks	Speaking Activities
six	• getting the main idea • identifying stressed words and reductions • guessing information from context	• describing and identifying a crime suspect • matching first aid instructions to illustrations	• retelling a radio report • giving advice about unsafe activities • describing an emergency • role playing calling for help
seven	• getting the main idea • identifying stressed words • recognizing tag question intonations • guessing information from context	• taking notes on telephone calls	• describing symptoms and giving advice • role playing making appointments with a doctor • role playing visiting a psychologist
eight	• getting the main idea • identifying stressed words • guessing information from context	• filling in missing information on a TV program guide	• summarizing a news report • describing/comparing programs • summarizing a movie plot • discussing censorship • role playing a disagreement
nine	• getting the main idea • identifying stressed words • recognizing intonation patterns of exclamation • guessing information from context	• gathering information for weekend activities	• describing personal characteristics • summarizing key elements of American football • comparing social customs • surveying people about finding a mate • giving/accepting compliments • role playing going to a video dating service
ten	• getting the main idea • identifying stressed words • guessing information from context	• planning a birthday party: matching tasks and people to do them	• talking about Thanksgiving • describing holidays/holiday plans • making, accepting, and refusing invitations • role playing a wedding-day surprise

Summary of Listening/Speaking Skills and Activities

Chapter	Listening Skills	Listening Tasks	Speaking Activities
eleven	• getting the main idea • identifying stressed words • guessing information from context	• following instructions to set a VCR clock	• discussing advantages/disadvantages of electric cars • interpreting a cartoon • discussing life without new technology • describing how to operate simple devices • role playing a disagreement
twelve	• getting the main idea • identifying stressed words • guessing information from context	• matching classified ads to items described • following directions in a department store	• summarizing advice about buying a used car • buying/selling items through classified ads • returning merchandise to a store • role playing catching a shoplifter

School Life

Useful Words and Expressions You will hear the following words and expressions in this chapter. If you are not sure what they mean, try to guess the meanings from the context.

How are you doing?
Stop by.
Can you give us an idea of . . . ?
What's the make of your car?
Call me at 555-0000.
Give me a call.
Pick it up.

a midterm exam
a snack bar
a gym
a T.A.
a chem class
a math class

PART one

Listening to Conversations

prelistening questions

1. Look at the picture below. What are the students doing?
2. What do you think they are talking about?

Getting the Main Idea

exercise 1

Jack, Peter, and Herb are new students at Faber College. They meet in the student lounge of their dormitory. Close your book and listen to their conversation. You may not understand every word. Listen for the main ideas.

exercise 2

Now you will hear five questions about the conversation. Listen to the questions. Then write answers to the questions on the lines below. Discuss your answers with your classmates.

1. _____

2. _____

3. _____

4. _____

5. _____

Stress

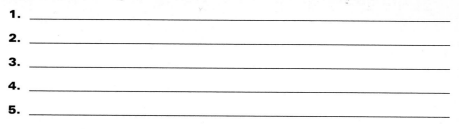

In spoken English, important words are *stressed*. This means that they are spoken *louder, longer,* or *higher* than other (unstressed) words. Stressed words usually give the most important information.

examples: My na′me is To′m.
　　　　　　 We're on the sa′me flo′or.

exercise 3

Now listen to the first part of the conversation again. Some of the stressed words are missing. Repeat each sentence during the pause. Then fill in the missing stressed words.

doing	right	accent (*two times*)
Texas	Peter (*three times*)	meet
Peter Riley	Jack	you're
name	Herb (*two times*)	think
roommate	hi (*two times*)	

JACK: _____ ! How're you _____?

PETER: Oh, hi! You're _____ , right?

JACK: That's _____ . What's your _____ again?

PETER: _____ . _____ _____ .

JACK: _____ , this is my _____ , _____ .

PETER: _____ , _____ .

HERB: Nice to _____ you.

PETER: Are you from _____ ?

HERB: Yeah. Why? Do you _____ I have an _____ ?

PETER: Yeah.

HERB: Ha! _____ the ones with the _____ !

exercise 4

Now listen to the rest of the conversation. Mark the stressed words as in the example.

JACK: Lísten, Peter. We're really húngry. Do you want to get something to eát with us?

PETER: I can't. I have to meet my new roommate.

HERB: Oh, yeah? Well, okay. Listen, stop by and see us. We're up in 212.

PETER: Hey, we're on the same floor. Room 220.

HERB AND JACK: Great!

PETER: Okay. See you guys later.

HERB AND JACK: See you.

Reductions

> In spoken English, important words are usually stressed. Many words that are not stressed are often *reduced.*
>
> *examples:* Do you . . . → D'ya . . .
> How are you doing? → How're ya doing?

exercise 5

Listen to these examples of reductions from the conversation. Repeat them after the speaker.

Note: The underlined forms are not acceptable spellings in written English.

reduction	long form
Hi! How're ya doing?	Hi! How are you doing?
Peter, this's my roommate, Herb.	Peter, this is my roommate, Herb.
Nice ta meetcha.	Nice to meet you.
Are ya from Texas?	Are you from Texas?
D'ya wanna get something to eat with us?	Do you want to get something to eat with us?
I hafta meet my new roommate.	I have to meet my new roommate.

exercise 6 Listen to the reductions in these sentences. Write the long forms in the blanks. You may want to repeat the sentences for pronunciation practice.

1. _____ _____ _____ feeling?

2. _____ _____ in an hour.

3. Jack, _____ _____ _____

   _____ eat at the cafeteria?

4. When _____ _____ _____

   _____ meet your roommate?

Pronunciation of the -*s* Ending

> The -*s* ending is pronounced three ways, according to the end of the word:
>
> • /iz/ after -*ch*, -*sh*, -*s*, -*x*, and -*z* endings.
>
>   *examples:* teaches, uses, boxes
>
> • /s/ after voiceless -*p*, -*t*, -*k*, or -*f* endings.
>
>   *examples:* drinks, speaks, hits
>
> • /z/ after voiced consonant endings.
>
>   *examples:* carries, brings, runs

exercise 7 Listen to the following words. Check the sound you hear. The first one is done as an example.

	/s/	/iz/	/z/		/s/	/iz/	/z/
1. plays	☐	☐	☑	**5.**	☐	☐	☐
2.	☐	☐	☐	**6.**	☐	☐	☐
3.	☐	☐	☐	**7.**	☐	☐	☐
4.	☐	☐	☐	**8.**	☐	☐	☐

exercise 8 Answer the following questions in complete sentences. Pay attention to the pronunciation of the -*s* endings.

1. Where does your teacher work?
2. What does he or she teach?
3. Does your teacher give you homework?
4. When does your class begin?
5. When does it end?

PART two
Summarizing Main Ideas

exercise 1

You are going to listen to a short speech. You may not understand every word. Before you listen, think about these questions:

1. Who is speaking?
2. Who is listening to the speech?
3. Where are they?

Now listen to the speech.

exercise 2

What information did the speaker give in the speech? Circle *yes* or *no*.

1. Welcome to Faber College.   yes   no
2. Faber is a great school.   yes   no
3. We hope you like it.   yes   no
4. A campus tour begins   yes   no
   in fifteen minutes.

If you answered *yes* to all statements, you understood the *main* or *important* ideas. *Remember:* You don't need to understand all the words to understand the main message.

Now listen to the full speech again. Focus on the main ideas only.

exercise 3

Later on the campus tour, one of the students asks the tour guide this question: "Can you give us an idea of some good places to eat?" Listen to the guide's answer. Write the key words. The answer has two parts.

Part A, key words: _____

_____

_____

_____

Part B, key words: _____

_____

_____

_____

exercise 4 With a classmate, summarize each part of the guide's answer in short, simple sentences. Use the key words from Exercise 3.

Part A: _____

_____

_____

Part B: _____

_____

_____

PART three
Guessing Information

focus on testing

When you listen to people talking, you may not understand all the words. However, you can use the words you do know—and the context of the conversation—to help you guess the words you do not know. Guessing information is an important listening skill. It can also help you do well on standardized listening tests, such as the TOEFL. The following exercises will help you practice this skill.

Jack, Peter, and Kenji are talking. Listen to their conversation. The conversation has five parts, with a question at the end of each part. When you hear a question, circle the correct answer a, b, or c below. Then listen to the next part of the conversation, which contains the correct answer to the previous question. The first one is done as an example.

1. a. at a horse race
    b. at the bookstore
    c. at a pizza restaurant *(circled)*

2. a. another student in their class
    b. their chemistry professor
    c. the teaching assistant in their chemistry class

3. a. It's a little unusual.
    b. It's terrible.
    c. It's fun.

4. a. at the recreation center only
    b. on the telephone
    c. by paying $5

5. a. Kenji will reserve a tennis court.
    b. Peter will lose his lunch.
    c. The four boys will play tennis together.

PART four
Listening Tasks

Peter and Kenji have an answering machine. When they are not home, the machine records telephone messages for them. Listen to the people who call. Are they friends? Classmates? Parents? What are they calling about? Who gets more messages, Peter or Kenji? Complete the form for each message with the important information. The first one is done as an example.

TELEPHONE MESSAGE:

For _Kenji_

Caller _Dr. Brown_

Phone _855 - 7962_

Area Code Number Extension

☐ Telephoned   ☑ Please call back

☐ Returned your call   ☐ Will call back

Message: _Change appointment from Tues. → Wed. 2:00_

1.

TELEPHONE MESSAGE:

For _Peter_

Caller _Mandi_

Phone _557 4906_

Area Code Number Extension

☐ Telephoned   ☐ Please call back

☐ Returned your call   ☐ Will call back

Message: _Any time before 11:00 pm call me. pls_

2.

TELEPHONE MESSAGE:

For _peter_

Caller _Bod_

Phone _3813644_ _Chris house_

Area Code Number Extension

☐ Telephoned   ☐ Please call back

☐ Returned your call   ☐ Will call back

Message: _Michell pelfers_

3.

TELEPHONE MESSAGE:

For _Kenji_

Caller _Mr Returns_

Phone _____ 4745_
      Area Code   Number   Extension

☐ Telephoned   ☐ Please call
                          back

☑ Returned your   ☐ Will call back
  call

Message: _School office still able_
transfer to need it
very slow
Don't have transcry

4.

TELEPHONE MESSAGE:

For _Peter_

Caller _Dick_

Phone _Penny library_
      Area Code   Number   Extension

☐ Telephoned   ☐ Please call
                          back

☐ Returned your   ☐ Will call back
  call

Message: _____
ask for Grace or Dick
Biological book

5.

TELEPHONE MESSAGE:

For _Peter_

Caller _Kevin Cullen_

Phone _Kevin 278 1926_
      Area Code   Number   Extension

☐ Telephoned   ☐ Please call
                          back

☐ Returned your   ☐ Will call back
  call

Message: _is available_
how much you charge
for tutoring math

6.

TELEPHONE MESSAGE:

For _Kenji_

Caller _Autos Garage car_

Phone _____
      Area Code   Number   Extension

☐ Telephoned   ☐ Please call
                          back

☐ Returned your   ☐ Will call back
  call

Message: _28 dollar since_
charge 1:30 m
pick up.

Herb calls the college about a parking permit and talks to a secretary. Listen to the conversation and complete the application below.

PARKING PERMIT APPLICATION

Faber College

Name: _____

         Last   *First*   *Middle Initial*

Address: _____

Phone: _____

Car: _____

        Make   *Model*   *Year*

License Plate: _____

Fall Semester ☐   Amount enclosed $ _____

Spring Semester ☐

All year ☐

PART five
Speaking Activities

Making Introductions. In this activity you will introduce classmates to each other.

1. Sit in a circle if possible.
2. Write your first name on a card and put the card on your desk for everyone to see.
3. Ask a student next to you three or four questions like these:
   a. Where are you from?
   b. What do you do?
   c. Do you work?
   d. Do you have a hobby?

4. Now introduce your partner to several other students in the class.

> example: Jose, this is Noriko. Noriko, this is Jose. Jose is from Mexico. He is here to study engineering.

5. Put away your name cards. Go around the room and see how many names you remember. If you can't remember someone's name, use expressions like these:

> Excuse me, what's your name again?
> I'm sorry, can you tell me your name again?
> I'm sorry, I don't remember your name.
> You're Noriko, right?

activity **2**

Body Language.   In Part One, Jack introduces Herb to Peter. Look at their picture on page 2 and tell what "body language" Herb and Peter are using. Are they looking directly at each other? Are they standing far apart? Now discuss what the following gestures mean in the United States. Do they mean the same in your culture?

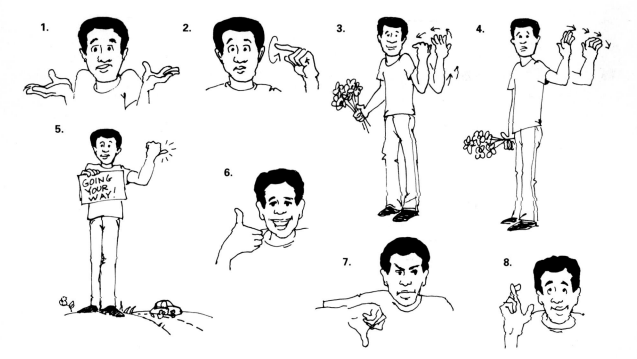

3. Use body language to show the following situations.
   a. You don't know the answer to the question.
   b. You think that the class is boring.
   c. You can't hear what someone is saying.
   d. Someone on the phone is talking too much.

Role Play.   Joe and Naomi are students at the same college. They meet for the first time at the student cafeteria when their trays collide. What do they say? How do they feel? Will they meet again?

Prepare a conversation with a partner. Memorize your lines and put on a skit for the class.

CHAPTER two

Experiencing Nature

in this chapter

Useful Words and Expressions You will hear the following words and expressions in this chapter. If you are not sure what they mean, try to guess the meanings from the context.

The weather is going to clear up.	How was the weather?
What's the weather like?	Celsius (Fahrenheit)
I'm worn out.	It's 13 below.
The weather is going to warm up.	in the high (low) seventies
I don't mind (the heat).	lows
What's it like out?	mid-fifties
I think I'll pass. (No, thanks.)	highs

DID YOU KNOW?

- **National Parks cover about 3 percent of the total land area in the United States.**
- **The average American throws away almost 1,300 pounds of garbage a year.**
- **The largest park in North America is Wood Buffalo National Park in Alberta, Canada. It was established in 1922 and covers more than 17,000 square miles.**

PART **one**
Listening to Conversations

prelistening questions

1. Look at the picture. Where do you think the students are going?
2. Why do some people like to go camping?
3. Where will the three boys sleep?
4. Why might camping be dangerous?

Getting the Main Idea

exercise 1

Peter, Herb, and a friend, Mike, are going camping for the weekend. They are having a conversation in the car. Close your book and listen to their conversation. You may not understand every word. Listen for the main ideas.

exercise 2

Now you will hear six questions about the conversation. Listen to the questions. Then write answers to the questions on the lines below. Discuss your answers with your classmates.

1. _____

2. _____

3. _____

4. _____

5. _____

6. _____

Stress

> Remember, stressed words usually give the main idea and are pronounced *louder, longer,* and *higher* than unstressed words.

exercise 3

Now listen to the first part of the conversation again. Repeat each sentence during the pause. Then fill in the missing stressed words.

real	dry	kinds
bad	hot (*two times*)	funny
cowboys	traffic	this
snows	winter	summer
hate	egg	skiing
nothing	raining	

PETER: I _____ to drive in _____ like this.

MIKE: Especially when it's _____ .

HERB: You think _____ is _____ ? Back in Texas a little rain

like this is _____ !

PETER: Really? Isn't Texas _____ and _____ ?

HERB: Oh, we have all _____ of weather in Texas. In the

_____ it's so _____ you can fry an _____

on the street. And in the _____ it _____ in some

places.

MIKE: Well, you never see pictures of _____ _____ .

HERB: Ha ha! _____ _____ .

exercise 4  Now listen to the rest of the conversation. Mark the stressed words.

MIKE: Bóy, this róad is nárrow. Be cáreful! We don't want to spend the week in the hospital.

HERB: So when do you think we'll get to Bald Mountain?

PETER: Not before midnight.

HERB: Then let's stay in a motel tonight.

PETER: Yeah, it doesn't look like the weather is going to clear up.

MIKE: And I'm not sleeping out in the woods until I hear the weather report.

can vs. *can't*

> Notice the contrast between the verb forms *can* and *can't* in the follow-ing sentences.
>
> I can méet you tomorrow.
>
> I can't méet you tomorrow.
>
> *Can* is unstressed, so the vowel is reduced.
> *Can't* is stressed, so the vowel is not reduced.

exercise 5 Now listen to and repeat each statement. Circle *yes* if the statement is affirmative and *no* if the statement is negative. The first one is done as an example.

1. yes (no)
2. yes no
3. yes no
4. yes no
5. yes no

6. yes no
7. yes no
8. yes no
9. yes no
10. yes no

Reductions

> Remember that words that are not stressed are often reduced.
>
> *examples:* Want to . . . → Wanna . . . ?
>
> Going to → Gonna?

 **exercise 6**

Listen to these examples of reductions from the conversation. Repeat them after the speaker.

reduction	long form
We 'ave all <u>kindza</u> weather in Texas.	We have all kinds of weather in Texas.
When <u>d'ya</u> think we'll get to Bald Mountain?	When do you think we'll get to Bald Mountain?
We don't <u>wanna</u> spend the week in the hospital.	We don't want to spend the week in the hospital
It doesn't look like the weather is <u>gonna</u> clear up.	It doesn't look like the weather is going to clear up.

 exercise 7

Listen to the reductions in the following conversation. Write the long forms in the blanks. You may want to repeat the sentences for pronunciation practice.

PETER: What _____ _____ _____ in the car?

GAIL: We _____ all _____ _____ stuff.

PETER: _____ _____ have any drinks?

GAIL: Sure. What _____ _____ _____

_____ have?

PETER: How _____ _____ Coke?

PART two
Summarizing Main Ideas

 **exercise 1**

Peter, Mike, and Herb are at a motel. They see a man and a woman talking to the manager. The man and the woman look tired but excited. Listen to their story.

> *Note:* In informal, spoken English, people sometimes use the simple present tense to tell a story about the recent past.

exercise 2

Now you will hear just the key sentences of the same story. As you listen, look at the key verbs below. Take notes to help you retell the story. Don't try to copy complete sentences. For example after the verb hike, you might write man and woman hike in rain.

1. hike: _____

2. go:_____

   change: _____

3. can't find: _____

4. see: _____

5. wear:_____

6. scare: _____

exercise 3

Listen to the story again if necessary. Then try to tell the story to a classmate in your own words. Use the key words from Exercise 2.

PART three
Guessing Information

focus on testing

Peter, Mike, and Herb are camping in the woods. Listen to their conversation. When you hear a question, circle the correct answer. Then listen to the next part of the conversation, which will contain the correct answer to the previous question.

1. a. He is fishing.
   b. He is cooking a fish.
   c. He is telling a secret.

2. a. They're hungry.
   b. They're angry.
   c. They're tired.

3. a. It's enjoyable.
   b. It's uncomfortable.
   c. It's boring.

4. a. to the top of a mountain
   b. to a place for lunch
   c. to the valley

5. a. Shoot a gun.
   b. Take photographs.
   c. Send postcards.

Homework

PART four
Listening Tasks

activity 1

Mike is listening to the weather forecast on the radio. Listen to the information and use the chart to take notes about the weekend weather.

5:00 PM — Part ?

	FRIDAY	SATURDAY	SUNDAY
Sky (cloudy? fair?)	*Prrt.? cloudy*	*fair*	*fair*
Temperature		*L*	
High	*61°*	*60°*	*70°*
Low	*50%*	*45° night*	*50°*
Rain (yes? no?)	*Sommes yes*		

50% chance on Rain on Monday

activity 2

Listen to the following conversations about the weather. Write the key words that help you know what season it is. Then write the name of the season. The first one is done as an example.

1. Clues: nice surprise, usually cooler, brown leaves
   Season: fall
2. Clues: *Low -30° I am going to the corner store take your coat it is freeze outside*
   Season: *winter*
3. Clues: *Rain nice to tree & lifes will goes to the trees and flower coming back to the trees again*
   Season: *Spring*
4. Clues: *Humidities, drinks take drinks somes where*
   Season: *Summer*

activity 3

Listen to more conversations about the weather. Circle the temperature you hear.

1. 19   (95)   99
2. (80)   18   8
3. 13   30   (30s)
4. 14   (40)   44
5. (103)   130   133
6. 30s   (30)   13
7. (-13)   30   3
8. 70   (70s)   17

PART five
Speaking Activities

activity **1**   **Seasons.** What activities do you think about when you think of winter? Spring? Summer? Fall? Look at the chart below. Ask a partner about the weather and activities in New York during different seasons.

example: What's the weather like in New York during the spring?
           What sport is popular in the fall?

United States: New York

Winter (Jan./Feb.)	Spring (Mar./Apr./May)	Summer (June/July/Aug.)	Fall (Sept./Oct.)	Winter (Nov./Dec.)
Weather				
cold	warm	hot	cool	cool
snowy	cool	humid	windy	cold
rainy	rainy	sunny	rainy	rainy
cloudy				
gray				
Things to Do				
ski	plant flowers	go to beach	walk in park	skate
skate	walk	swim		walk in park
	bike ride	travel		
		go on vacation		
		picnic		
		barbecue		
Sports				
hockey	basketball	baseball	football	football
Major Holidays				
New Year's Day	Easter	Memorial Day	Labor Day	Thanksgiving
Presidents' Day		Fourth of July	Columbus Day	Christmas

 **activity 2**   **Seasons in Your Home Country.** Think about your home country or city. Fill in the second chart. Explain it to a partner from a different country. If your country has different seasons, make changes to the chart.

Your Country: _____

Winter (Jan./Feb.)	Spring (Mar./Apr./ May)	Summer (June/July/ Aug.)	Fall (Sept./Oct.)	Winter (Nov./Dec.)
Weather *Cold* Rainy, Snowy, gray.	*very* Cool nice			
Things to Do -Walk. swimmg.				
Sports Swimming. soccer.				
Major Holidays 3 New Year			Ramadan	

Discussing Sports. Sit in small groups. Choose one of the sports below. Describe the sport but don't mention its name. Let the other students guess which sport you are talking about. Use *can* and *can't* with the correct stress.

example: You can do this sport in all seasons, but it's more popular in the summer. Most children can do it, but sometimes it can be dangerous. You can do it outdoors or indoors, and you don't need any special equipment, just a bathing suit. You can do it by yourself, but you can't do it outside the water! (*Answer:* swimming)

When each person in the group has described a sport, describe other sports that you know about.

 **activity 4**   **Discussing the Environment.**   Talk about the following questions in groups of three or four.

1. What kinds of pollution (dirty air, water) are common in your home country? Who/what causes them?
2. Is recycling (of glass, plastic, or paper) popular there?
3. Interview three people outside of class and find out about their own recycling habits. Then report back to the class. Use the chart below as a guide. Add questions of your own.

Recycling Habits

	Person 1	Person 2	Person 3
1. What things do you recycle at home?			
2. How often do you recycle?			
3. Does your community make it easy or difficult for you to recycle?			
How?			
4. Do you recycle at work?			
If yes, what kinds of things?			
Other Questions:			
5.			
6.			

Role Play.   George and his younger brother Lou are leaving their campsite in a mess. Rick is a park ranger. His job is to protect the natural beauty and cleanliness of the park. Rick stops the campers to explain their responsibilities to them. In groups of two or three, play the roles of Rick, George, and Lou. The following expressions and idioms may help you express your ideas. Your teacher can explain them.

EXPLAINING RULES

You need to. . . .
You shouldn't. . . .
It's against the rules to. . . .
You're not allowed to. . . .
You'd better. . . .

APOLOGIZING

I'm (we're) sorry.
Excuse me (us).
You're absolutely right.
I (we) won't let it happen again.

CHAPTER three

Living to Eat or Eating to Live?

in this chapter

Useful Words and Expressions You will hear the following words and expressions in this chapter. If you are not sure what they mean, try to guess the meanings from the context.

a grocery list	for sale
a checkbook	a shopping cart
an express line	diet
groceries	lose weight
a sale	gain weight
a fast-food place	calories
a barbecue	the counter
on sale	

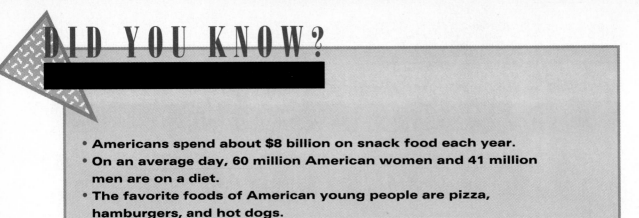

- Americans spend about $8 billion on snack food each year.
- On an average day, 60 million American women and 41 million men are on a diet.
- The favorite foods of American young people are pizza, hamburgers, and hot dogs.

PART one

Listening to Conversations

prelistening questions

1. Look at the picture. What kinds of things are the customers buying?
2. What are the people at the cashier's stand going to do next?
3. Who shops for groceries in your family?

Getting the Main Idea

exercise 1

Mr. and Mrs. Nutley are doing their weekly grocery shopping. Close your book and listen to their conversation. You may not understand every word. Listen for the main ideas.

exercise 2

Now you will hear six questions about the conversation. Listen to the questions. Then write answers to the questions on the lines below. Discuss your answers with your classmates.

1. _Because he was hungry_
2. _Ninety-nine cents_
3. _No_
4. _Is expensive_
5. _For my yes_
6. _No they are not._

Stress

exercise 3

Listen to the first part of the conversation again. Repeat each sentence during the pause. Remember to pronounce stressed words *louder, longer,* and *higher.* Then fill in the missing stressed words.

_ why	= see (*two times*)	— hungry
— that	— cents	— strawberries
—do	aren't	—shopping
_ fresh	_ cookies	—have
—always	— like	_ got
— grocery	—things	
—nice	—army	

MR. N: Well, dear, I _____ _got_ _____ a few _____ _things_ _____ that _____ _aren't_ _____ on the _____ _grocery_ _____ list.

MRS. N: I can _____ _see_ _____ _____ _that_ _____ ! You're not _____ _shopping_ _____ for an _____ _army_ _____ , you know.

MR. N: You know I _____ _always_ _____ _____ _do_ _____ this when I'm hungry.

MRS. N: Well, let's _____ _see_ _____ what you _____ _have_ _____ here.

MR. N: Some _____ _nice_ _____ , _____ _fresh_ _____ _____ _strawberries_ _____ for only ninety-nine _____ _cents_ _____ .

MRS. N: Well, that's okay. But _____ _why_ _____ do you have all these _____ _cookies_ _____ ?

MR. N: I don't know; don't you _____ _like_ _____ them?

exercise 4 Now listen to the rest of the conversation. Mark the stressed words.

MRS. N: Oh, I suppose. I hope you have a box of soap here.

MR. N: Sure—a large one.

MRS. N: That steak looks really expensive!

MR. N: Well, it isn't. It's just three dollars a pound.

MRS. N: What's this? More ice cream? We already have a gallon at home. Put it back and hand me my checkbook.

CASHIER: I'm sorry, ma'am. This is the express line. You have too many groceries, and we don't take checks here.

Teens or Tens?

Notice the differences in stress between the following pairs of words. In the numbers 13 to 19, stress the syllable *-teen* as well as the first syllable. For 20, 30, 40, etc., to 90, stress the first syllable only.

thirteen thirty   fourteen forty   eighteen eighty

exercise 5 Listen to these sentences. Write the number you hear on the blank line in each picture. The first one is done as an example.

Reductions

Listen to these examples of reductions from the conversation. Repeat them after the speaker.

reduction	long form
Let's see whatcha have here.	Let's see what you have here.
Why d'ya have all these cookies?	Why do you have all these cookies?
I dunno.	I don't know.
Doncha like 'em?	Don't you like them?

Listen to the reductions in the following conversation. Write the long forms in the blanks. You may want to repeat the sentences for pronunciation practice.

CUSTOMER: Waiter?

WAITER: Yes, sir. Do you know _____ _____ want?

CUSTOMER: _____ _____ have any fresh whitefish?

WAITER: Yes, we catch _____ fresh every day.

CUSTOMER: Great, I'll have some.

WAITER: What kind of wine _____ _____ want with that?

CUSTOMER: I _____ _____ . Why _____

_____ recommend something?

WAITER: Our California wines are excellent.

PART two
Summarizing Main Ideas

exercise 1 Many Americans worry about how much they weigh. In fact, about a third of the American people are overweight, and this number is increasing. Listen to the following advice about losing weight. Take notes on the do's and don'ts.

Do	Don't

Work with a partner. Compare your notes. Using complete sentences, summarize the advice you heard on the tape. Can you think of some additional advice about dieting?

exercise 2 Kenji and his friends are shopping at the Shop-and-Save Department Store. They hear some announcements. Before you listen, talk with a partner about what kind of things stores announce to their shoppers—for example, special sales, store hours, etc. Then listen to the tape.

 **exercise 3** Listen to the announcements again. Write down the important information. Don't copy sentences; just write your notes below.

New hours: _____

Special sale: _____

Sportswear: _____

Parking: _____

Food: _____

Little boy: _____

PART **three**
Guessing Information

focus on testing

In this section, you will hear four conversations. As you listen to each one, decide where the people are eating and circle the correct answer. Then listen to the next conversation, which contains the correct answer to the previous question.

1. a. coffee shop
   b. cafeteria
   c. nice restaurant

2. a. fast-food place
   b. coffee shop
   c. expensive restaurant

3. a. cafeteria
   b. nightclub
   c. fast-food place

4. a. nice restaurant
   b. cafeteria
   c. fast-food place

PART four
Listening Tasks

activity 1

Tom is teaching Kenji how to cook. Listen to the recipe for French toast and take notes.

INGREDIENTS:

_____

_____

_____

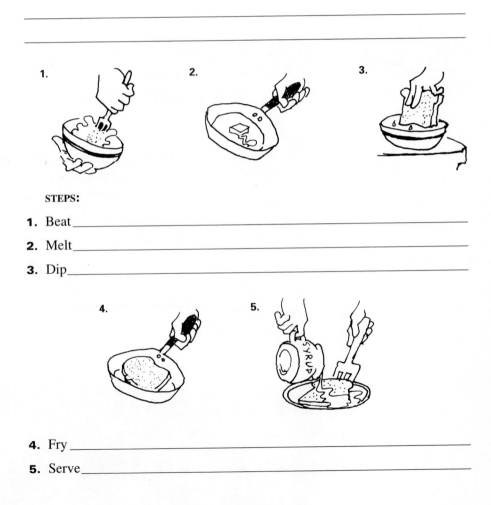

1.

2.

3.

STEPS:

1. Beat _____

2. Melt _____

3. Dip _____

4.

5.

4. Fry _____

5. Serve _____

activity 2   Mr. and Mrs. Nutley plan to drive around the United States soon. Their niece, Paula, is a chef. She tells them about foods popular in different parts of the country. Take a look at the map below of the United States and Canada. As you hear the name of each food, write it on the map in the place where it is popular.

PART five
Speaking Activities

activity 1   **Comparing Eating Habits.**   Compare each pair of items below by
making a list of the differences. Then discuss each topic with a partner. (If
you've never been to North America, compare your home country with another
place you've visited.)

COMPARE

1. your eating habits now   and   in your home country

   _____   _____

   _____   _____

2. the price of food in North
   America   and   in your home country

   _____   _____

   _____   _____

3. the time and size of meals in
   North America   and   in your home country

   _____   _____

   _____   _____

4. restaurants in North America   and   in your home country

   _____   _____

   _____   _____

5. table manners in North
   America   and   in your home country

   _____   _____

   _____   _____

Planning a Barbecue.   A typical American barbecue is an outdoor meal in which meat, chicken, or fish is cooked over an open fire. Discuss the following questions with a group of your classmates.

1. Do people in your home country cook and eat outdoors?
2. If so, on what occasions?
3. What foods are served at a barbecue in your country?

Plan an American barbecue with a partner. The two lists below contain all the things you will need. Person A looks only at list A. Person B looks only at list B. Ask questions using *some* and *any* to find all the things on the other person's list. Write these items in the blanks on your list.

examples: Person A: Do you have any onions?
Person B: No, I don't have any.
Person A: Do you have some ketchup?
Person B: Yes, I have a bottle of ketchup.

LIST A

Supplies

plates

plastic cups

charcoal

_____

_____

_____

Beverages

Coke

beer

coffee

_____

_____

_____

Food

potato chips

hot dogs

chicken

green salad

mustard

watermelon

_____

_____

_____

_____

_____

LIST B

Supplies	*Food*
plastic knives and forks	cheese
napkins	hamburgers
matches	potato salad
_____	ketchup
	ice cream
_____	cake
_____	_____
Beverages	_____
iced tea	_____
wine	_____
juice	_____
_____	_____
_____	_____

Now decide on a list of guests together. Finally, decide how much of each item on the list you will need to serve your guests.

activity 3 **Teaching a Recipe.** Teach your class a simple recipe from your country. First, list the ingredients. Then describe each step. Use Part Four, Activity 1 as a model. Suggest that your classmates take notes while you speak. Then invite some of them to read back the recipe from their notes.

activity 4 **Role Play.** Cathy is expecting dinner guests tonight. She has found everything she needs at the supermarket. She is ready to pay, but she can't find her wallet. What can she do? What will she do?

Prepare a conversation with one or two partners. Memorize your lines and put on a skit for the class. The following expressions and idioms may help you express your ideas.

I'll be back in ten minutes	Never mind.	Could you lend me . . . ?
Forget it.	Oh, darn!	Can I borrow . . . ?

CHAPTER four

Getting Around the Community

in this chapter

Useful Words and Expressions You will hear the following words and expressions in this chapter. If you are not sure what they mean, try to guess the meanings from the context.

to get a haircut
to get around
to get on
to get off
a dry-cleaning shop

How long does it take?
Turn right. (left)
How do I get there?
Make a right. (left)

- The longest traffic jam on record happened on February 16, 1980. It stretched over 109 miles from Lyons, France, toward Paris.
- São Paulo, Brazil, has more buses than any city in the world— over 10,000! (Mexico City has the most taxis, about 60,000.)
- The New York City subway system has more than 230 miles of tracks and over 470 subway stations.

PART **one**

Listening to Conversations

prelistening questions

1. Look at the picture. What are Herb and Mike doing?
2. What are some easy ways to get around in a city?
3. What do you enjoy doing in big cities?

Getting the Main Idea

exercise 1

Herb and Mike live in a small college town near a big city. Mike is going into the city today. Close your book and listen to their conversation. You may not understand every word. Listen for the main ideas.

exercise 2

Now you will hear five questions about the conversation. Listen to the questions. Then write answers to the questions on the lines below. Discuss your answers with your classmates.

1. _No he is bussy he goes to the city. and duy many things_
2. _becuse he needs to open checu account go to the bank Send Prackeqe ot Poste of liee_
3. _iu downtown_
4. _by taxi_
5. _nothing_

Stress

> Remember that stressed words usually express the main idea and are pronounced *louder, longer,* and *higher* than the unstressed words.

exercise 3

Listen to the first part of the conversation again. Repeat each sentence during the pause. Then fill in the missing stressed words.

sure	things	package	take	what
traffic	city	can't	might	around
bad	give	bank	back	like
math	help	much	taxi	

HERB: Say, Mike. Can you ____give____ me some ___help____ with my ____Mudho____ homework this afternoon?

MIKE: Umm, I'd ____like____ to, but I really ____can't____. I have to go into the ____City____ and do a lot of ____things____.

HERB: Oh yeah? Like ____what____?

MIKE: I have to go to the ____BANK____ and open a checking account, I have to mail a ____Package____ at the post office, and I ____might____ get a haircut too.

HERB: Well, that's not ____Such____. When are you going to come ____back____?

MIKE: I'm not ____Sure____. I might eat downtown if the ____traffic.____ looks ____bad____.

HERB: How are you going to get ____around____?

MIKE: I don't know. I think I'll ____take____ a ____taxi____.

exercise 4 Now listen to the rest of the conversation. Mark the stressed words.

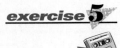

HERB: Why don't you take the bus; it's much cheaper.

MIKE: Maybe I will. Can I get you anything?

HERB: Let me see. . . . Could you get me some stamps?

MIKE: Sure.

HERB: And would you buy me some tennis balls?

MIKE: . . . Okay.

HERB: Oh, yeah . . . and our camping pictures are ready. Would you pick them up if you can?

MIKE: Is that all, boss?

HERB: Yes, for now.

Reductions

Remember that words which are *not* stressed are often reduced.

example: would you → wouldja.

exercise 5 Listen to these examples of reductions from the conversation. Repeat them after the speaker.

reduction	long form
Kinya gimme some help?	Can you give me some help?
I'd liketa, but I can't.	I'd like to, but I can't.
I hafta go into the city and do a lotta things.	I have to go into the city and do a lot of things.
Whenaya gonna come back?	When are you going to come back?
Howaya gonna get around?	How are you going to get around?
Can I getcha anything?	Can I get you anything?
Couldja get me some stamps?	Could you get me some stamps?
And wouldja buy me some tennis balls?	And would you buy me some tennis balls?
Pick 'em up if you can.	Pick them up if you can.

exercise 6

Listen to the reductions in the following conversation. Write the long forms in the blanks. You may want to repeat the sentences for pronunciation practice.

ANA: ___Can___ ___you___ show me where the bus stops?

SUE: ___I___ ___like___ ___to___, but I really don't know. You'll ___have___ ___to___ ask someone else. Or I can ___get___ ___you___ some bus maps.

ANA: Forget it; you're ___going___ ___to___ be late.

SUE: No, I don't ___have___ ___to___ rush.

ANA: Okay. ___would___ ___you___ please get ___them___, then?

SUE: Sure. I'll ___pick___ ___them___ right up.

ANA: ___Could___ ___you___ bring an extra for my friend?

PART **two**
Summarizing Main Ideas

exercise 1

Mike is back after a long afternoon in the city. He looks tired and unhappy. Listen to his conversation with his friends.

exercise 2

Now listen again. List the good things and the bad things you hear about cities and towns. A few examples are already written in.

		GOOD THINGS		BAD THINGS
BIG CITIES	1.		1.	trafic
	2.	Make more money	2.	noise
	3.	good shopping	3.	Smoke
		Exiting busy amfms	4.	Dangerous
			5.	
			6.	
SMALL TOWNS	1.	quiet	1.	conservative
	2.	friendly	2.	
	3.	cheaping		
	4.	boring		

 **exercise 3** Listen to the conversation again if necessary. Then discuss in your own words the good and bad things about big cities and small towns. Use the key words from Exercise 2 and be sure to make complete sentences.

PART **three**
Guessing Information

focus on testing

Listen to the following conversations, which take place in different parts of the city. When you hear a question, circle the correct answer. Then listen to the next line of the conversation, which contains the correct answer to the previous question.

1. a. in a post office
    b. in a bank
    c. in a gas station

2. a. on a train
    b. in a taxi
    c. on a bus

3. a. at a clothing store
    b. at a dry-cleaner's
    c. at a coffee shop

4. a. getting a driver's license
    b. visiting the eye doctor
    c. taking a final exam

5. a. at the airport
    b. at a bank
    c. at a post office

PART four
Listening Tasks

activity 1

Mike is getting directions to various places in the city. Right now, he is at Joe's Diner on Columbus Street. Look at the map and follow the directions you hear. On the map, in the correct location, write the name of each place Mike goes to.

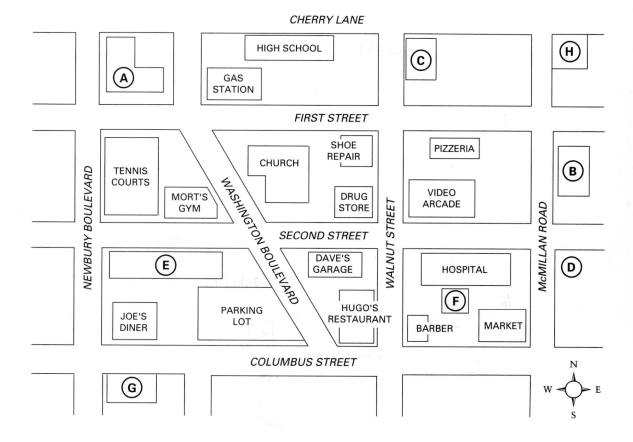

activity 2

If you need directions, your local bus company can help you. Just tell them where you want to leave from, where you want to go, and what time you need to get there. Listen to the following telephone conversations with the Metro Bus Company. Take notes on each conversation.

1. Destination: _____

   Bus number: _____

   Get on at (time): _____

   Get on at (place): _____

   Get off at (place): _____

2. Destination: _____

   Get on at (time): _____

   Get on at (place): _____

   Fare: _____

   Travel time: _____

3. Destination: _____

   Bus number: _____

   Get on at (place): _____

   Get off at (place): _____

   Bus runs how often: _____

PART **five**
Speaking Activities

activity 1

Asking For and Giving Directions. The following expressions are useful when asking or explaining how to go somewhere.

* How do I get to/find (the bank)?
* Go straight/north/south (on Main Street).
* Turn left/right (on First Avenue).
* Go through the intersection.
* Cross the street.
* Look for/you'll see (the supermarket) on the left/right (side of the street).

Look at the map on page 43. Work with a partner. Ask for directions to various places on the map.

> **example:** Q: How do I get from the hospital to the gas station?
> A: Go north on Walnut, turn left on First Street; you'll see the gas station on the corner of First and Washington Boulevard.

 **Your Neighborhood.** Describe your neighborhood to a partner. Use *there is, there are,* and *it's.* Here are some more useful expressions:

near / close to / not far from (my home)
across / on the other side of (the street, the river)
in the neighborhood

> **example:** My neighborhood is noisy but it's safe. There's a movie theater near my house. It's about three blocks away.

activity 3 **Comparing Types of Transportation.** In small groups discuss the kinds of transportation you used to use in your home town and those you use now. Take notes on the chart below. Make up some destinations of your own, if you wish. The following list of words and expressions may be helpful.

train	taxi	trolley
ferry	highway	local
car	bus	on foot
commute	express	street
streetcar	by bicycle	
subway	road	

	in my home town	now
to go to work		
to go to school		
to go to a friend's house		
to go to a food store		

Role Play.   Mr. Kim was in a hurry to buy a surprise birthday present. When he finished shopping, he got a surprise himself!

   With a partner, explain and discuss the cartoon, using the vocabulary below to help you. Then prepare and perform a funny skit about the situation. The following words and phrases may help you express your ideas.

EXPRESSIONS	PEOPLE	ADJECTIVES	OTHER
Oh, no?	police officer	forgetful	laws
I can't believe it?	meter maid	absentminded	regulations
What's going on?	parking officer	embarrassed	rules
Give me a break!			ticket
			citation

Home

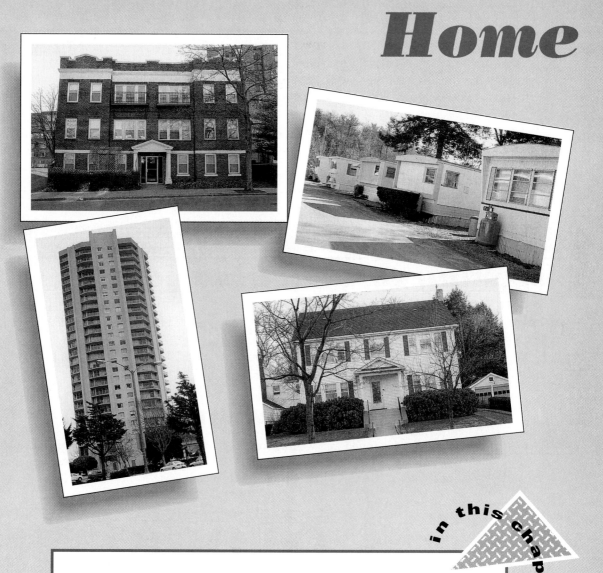

in this chapter

Useful Words and Expressions You will hear the following words and expressions in this chapter. If you are not sure what they mean, try to guess the meanings from the context.

It was a real pain.
Wow!
Everything is a mess.
I bet . . .
That's too bad.

to share a house
a leaking faucet
It's rented.
right away

DID YOU KNOW?

- **People in the United States typically spend about one week's take-home pay each month for rent.**
- **Sixty-four percent of homes in the United States are owned, not rented.**
- **The average number of people living in each home in the United States is 2.6**

PART one
Listening to Conversations

prelistening questions

1. How many times have you moved to a new house or apartment? What were the reasons for moving?
2. What is the best thing and the worst thing about your present house or apartment?

Getting the Main Idea

exercise 1

Peter and his friends are waiting for Mike at the cafeteria. Look at the picture and guess why Mike is late. Close your book and listen to their conversation. You may not understand every word. Listen for the main ideas.

exercise 2

Now you will hear seven questions about the conversation. Listen to the questions. Then write answers to the questions on the lines below. Discuss your answers with your classmates.

1. _____

2. _____

3. _____

4. _____

5. _____

6. _____

7. _____

Stress

exercise 3

Listen to the first part of the conversation again. Repeat each sentence during the pause. Remember to pronounce stressed words *louder, longer,* and *higher.* Then fill in the missing stressed words.

hour	moved	sorry
say	without	sister (*two times*)
decided	old	were
where	waited	apartment (*two times*)
five	corner	why

JUDY: So where _____ you? We _____ for an

_____ , but then we _____ to have lunch

_____ you.

MIKE: _____ , guys. I had to help my _____ move out of her

_____ _____ .

PETER: Did you _____ your _____ just _____ ?

MIKE: Yeah.

PETER: _____ was her _____ ?

MIKE: Right around the _____ . Just _____ minutes away.

_____ ?

exercise 4

Now listen to the rest of the conversation. Mark the stressed words.

PETER: My friend Bárbara needs a pláce right awáy. How bíg is it?

MIKE: It's a one-bedroom apartment with a small kitchen and bathroom. The living room has a fireplace.

PETER: Great! What did she pay there?

MIKE: Only six-fifty, but it might go up.

PETER: Could you give me the address for Barbara?

MIKE: Sure. It's 1213 Rose Avenue. Tell her to see the manager soon, before it's rented.

PETER: Okay. I'll call her right away.

Reductions

exercise 5

Listen to these examples of reductions from the conversation. Repeat them after the speaker.

reduction	long form
<u>Didja</u> say your sister moved?	Did you say your sister moved?
I <u>hadta</u> help.	I had to help.
She <u>hadta</u> get out.	She had to get out
I<u>' was</u> only six-fifty.	It was only six-fifty.
<u>Couldja gimme</u> the address?	Could you give me the address?
Tell <u>'er</u> to see the manager.	Tell her to see the manager.
I'll call <u>'er</u> right away.	I'll call her right away.

exercise 6

Listen to the reductions in the following conversation. Write the long forms in the blanks. You may want to repeat the sentences for pronunciation practice.

A: _____ _____ get your new phone yet?

B: Yeah, but I _____ _____ call the phone company three times. It was a real pain. Here's my new number. When you see Jane, _____ _____ _____ _____ my number, too?

A: Sure. I'll _____ _____ at school tomorrow.

Pronunciation of the -ed Ending

The -ed ending is pronounced three ways, according to the end of the word:

- /id/ after -d and -t endings.

  examples: waited, invited, needed

- /t/ after voiceless endings.

  examples: fixed, watched, helped

- /d/ after voiced consonant endings.

  examples: lived, showed, listened

exercise 7 Listen to the following words. Check the sound you hear. The first one is done as an example.

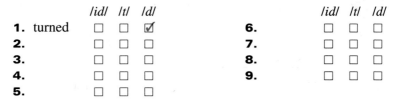

		/id/	/t/	/d/			/id/	/t/	/d/
1.	turned	☐	☐	☑	**6.**		☐	☐	☐
2.		☐	☐	☐	**7.**		☐	☐	☐
3.		☐	☐	☐	**8.**		☐	☐	☐
4.		☐	☐	☐	**9.**		☐	☐	☐
5.		☐	☐	☐					

exercise 8 Answer the following questions in complete sentences. Pay attention to the pronunciation of the -ed endings.

1. When did you move to this city?
2. Who recommended this school to you?
3. When did you start learning English?
4. When did you call your family?
5. When did you brush your teeth?

PART two
Summarizing Main Ideas

exercise 1 Barbara is looking at Marsha's old apartment. Listen as the manager shows Barbara around the apartment.

Listen again. Take notes about the good things and the bad things about the apartment. Two examples are already written in.

GOOD THINGS	BAD THINGS
1. new paint	1. *Higer rent*
2. *Diswasher*	2. *No air conditioning*
3. *All electric kichen*	3. *small bedroom*
4. *a big freezer*	4. higher rent
5. *new carpet*	5. *little Bedroom*
6. *big closets*	6. *noisy*
7. *Lights*	- *Ploming problems in the bathroom*
8. *fire place*	
9.	

exercise 3

Mr. Nutley passes Barbara on his way into his apartment. Listen to their conversation once. Then listen to it again and take notes.

Information about Mr. Nutley: *17 years they live there his marriel*

The neighborhood before: *Butiful parck alot kids they new everybody in the park*

The neighborhood now: *No body say Hello parking lot a lot of noise*

exercise 4

Work in groups of three. Take turns telling what the two people were talking about in your own words. Student A tells about Mr. Nutley, student B tells about the neighborhood before, and student C tells about the neighborhood now. Use your notes from Exercise 3.

PART three
Guessing Information

Mike's sister Marsha also found a new place to live. Listen to Mike and Marsha's conversation. Circle the correct answer to each question you hear. Then listen to the next part of the conversation, which gives you the correct answer to the previous question.

1. a. coffee
   b. magazines
   c. a pack of cigarettes

2. a. in the living room
   b. outside the house
   c. in the bedroom

3. a. It's very large.
   b. It isn't large.
   c. He couldn't find the bedroom.

4. a. a friend
   b. a dog
   c. a baby

5. a. because the rent was high.
   b. because the rent was low.
   c. because the rent was late.

PART four
Listening Tasks

activity 1

Barbara is going to move soon. She is calling the post office to tell them about her new address. A clerk is helping her fill out a change-of-address form. First, listen to the conversation, but don't write. Listen for the main ideas. Then listen to the conversation again. This time, complete the form with the information you hear.

	Print or Type (Last Name, First Name, Middle Initial)
OLD ADDRESS	No. and St., Apt., Suite or P.O. Box (In care of)
	City, State and ZIP Code
NEW ADDRESS	No. and St., Apt., Suite or P.O. Box (In care of)
	City, State and ZIP Code
	Effective Date
	Sign Here ▶

Signature & title of person authorizing address change (DO NOT print or type)

activity 2 It's moving day. Look at Barbara's empty new apartment. First, listen to her instructions to the movers. Then listen again. This time, write the number of the item in the correct place on the picture.

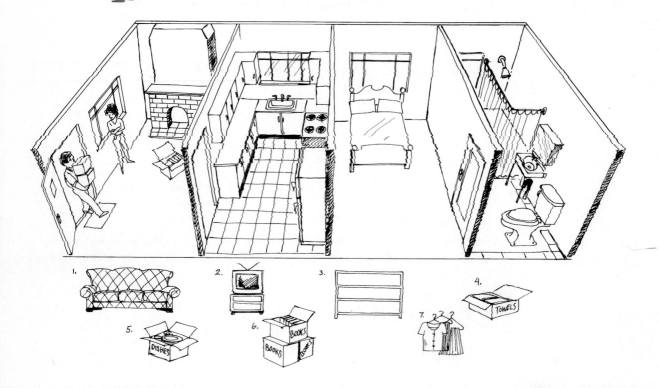

PART **five**
Speaking Activities

activity 1 **Renting an Apartment.** Here are three apartment ads; they do not give very much information. Make up at least five questions about each one to ask the manager.

1.

Beautiful apartment; walk to campus. Call 555-2009 for more information.

Rent? How much is the rent on leave

Number of rooms? How many Rooms

Noise? It is in the Calme Area Quiet

Stove/refrigerator? Does he stove and refrigerator

(Your own question) _____

2.

Two-bedroom apartment. $1000. Good location. Call 555-1828.

Area? _How ubant the Area._

Lease? _How long is the Lease_

Garage? __

Number of bathrooms? _How many bathrooms has the apart._

(Your own question) _____

3.

Roommate needed to share house. Lots of privacy. Leave message at 555-5520.

Male/female? _____

Number of rooms? _____

Smoking? _____

Location? _____

Rent? _____

Now work with a partner to apartment hunt. One of you is the manager, and the other one wants the apartment. Ask and answer the questions you have prepared. Change roles for each ad.

activity **2**

Moving Day. Working with a partner, look at the pictures below and on page 56 and tell a story about Marsha's moving day. Use the verbs below the pictures. Use the past tense and pronounce the *-ed* endings carefully. Listen to your partner's pronunciation as well.

example: Marsha **moved** into her house. The movers **carried** the boxes inside.

1.

move / carry / watch

2.

call / ask / describe

3.

look / decide

4.

unpack

5.

wash / drop

6.

dust / sneeze

Chapter Five • Home

7.

paint

8.

work / plant

9.

order

10.

rest

activity 3

Role Play.   Ali's rent just went up, so he wants to share his apartment with someone. Roberto wants to move out of his parents' house and is looking for a cheap place to live. Ali and Roberto meet at "Roommate Finders."

Prepare a conversation with a partner. Use expressions and idioms from this chapter. Then put on a skit about the situation.

The following words and phrases may help you express your ideas.

NOUNS	VERBS
smoker	to hunt for an apartment
non-smoker	to room with someone
	to split the rent
	to raise the rent

Emergencies and Strange Experiences

Useful Words and Expressions You will hear the following words and expressions in this chapter. If you are not sure what they mean, try to guess the meanings from the context.

to help out	heart attack
to call 911	x-ray
to be lost	flat tire
to be about to	flood
Richter Scale	Oops!

in this chapter

DID YOU KNOW?

- Accidents are the fourth largest cause of death in the United States.
- In the United States, the greatest number of accidents take place in Alaska, New Mexico, and Mississippi.
- Earthquakes are most common in the West, hurricanes in the East, and floods in the Midwest.

PART **one**
Listening to Conversations

prelistening questions

1. Look at the picture. What's happening?
2. Have you ever hurt yourself while playing a game?

Getting the Main Idea

exercise 1

Peter and Herb are finishing a game of tennis. Close your book and listen to their conversation. You may not understand every word. Listen for the main ideas.

 Now you will hear six questions about the conversation. Listen to the questions. Then write answers to the questions on the lines below. Discuss your answers with your classmates.

1. _____

2. _____

3. _____

4. _____

5. _____

6. _____

Stress

 Listen to the first part of the conversation again. Repeat each sentence during the pause. Remember to pronounce stressed words *louder, longer,* and *higher.* Then fill in the missing stressed words.

tried	hurt	broke
knee (*two times*)	fell	excuse
doctor	where	scream
leg	help	net
wrong	happened	playing

PETER: Nice game!

HERB: Oops . . . Ow—my _____ !

PETER: What's _____ ? _____ does it _____ ,

Herb?

HERB: My _____ . I think I _____ it.

WOMAN: _____ me, can I _____ ? I'm a _____ .

I was _____ over there when I heard you _____ .

What _____ ?

HERB: I _____ to jump over the _____ and I

_____ on my _____ .

exercise 4

Now listen to the rest of the conversation. Mark the stressed words.

WOMAN: Can you move it?

HERB: I don't think so, and it really hurts.

WOMAN: Let me have a look. Well, it may be broken.

PETER: Do you want me to go call 911?

WOMAN: No. There's a hospital right around the corner, so I don't think we'll need an ambulance. If you help me get your friend into my van, we can drive him over for some x-rays. The head of the emergency room is a friend of mine.

PETER: That's terrific. We're really lucky you were here!

HERB: We sure are. How can we thank you?

WOMAN: Oh, I'm always happy to help out. But after you're better, if you want to give me a tennis lesson. . . . Now let's get you up onto your good leg.

Reductions

Listen to these examples of reductions from the conversation. Repeat them after the speaker.

reduction	long form
I heardja scream.	I heard you scream.
I triedta jump over the net.	I tried to jump over the net.
Kinya move it?	Can you move it?
Lemme'ave a look.	Let me have a look.
We can drive'im over.	We can drive him over.
Now let's getcha up.	Now let's get you up.

exercise 6

Listen to the reductions in the following conversation. Write the long forms in the blanks. You may want to repeat the sentences for pronunciation practice.

NORIKO: I _____ _____ call you this morning. I

_____ _____ had an accident. Are you okay?

DEBBIE: Yeah, but my brother hurt his foot. I'll have to _____

_____ to school for a while.

NORIKO: That's too bad. Say! _____ _____

_____ _____ _____ a ride, too?

PART **two**
Summarizing the Main Ideas

exercise 1

You will hear a radio report about an earthquake. Discuss with a partner what kinds of information the report will probably give you. Then listen to the report.

exercise 2

Listen to the report again. Make up four questions about the earthquake report. Use the question words below.

1. What _____?

2. Where _____?

3. When _____?

4. How many _____?

exercise 3

Work with a partner. Take turns asking and answering your questions. Then use the answers to retell the radio report about the earthquake.

PART three
Guessing Information

focus on testing

Listen to the following conversations about emergencies. Decide what
each situation is, and circle the answer in your book. Then listen to the
next part of the conversation, which gives you the correct answer to the
previous question.

1. a. a fire
   b. a rainstorm
   c. an earthquake

2. a. a heart attack
   b. a car accident
   c. a broken leg

3. a. a flat tire
   b. a car accident
   c. an empty gas tank

4. a. The bus is late.
   b. The speakers lost their map.
   c. The speakers are lost.

5. a. an airplane crash
   b. a flood
   c. a boating accident

PART four
Listening Tasks

activity 1

Herb goes to a clinic for his knee. In the waiting room he overhears a police
officer talking to a woman and her companion. Listen to what they tell the
police officer.

Listen again. Complete the form with a description of the thief.

SUSPECT DESCRIPTION FORM

Sex: _____

Age: _____

Hair color: _____

Beard: yes ☐ no ☐   Moustache: yes ☐ no ☐

Height:_____

Weight: _____

Clothing: _____

_____

Special marks: _____

 activity 3

Now look at the men in the police station in the drawing. With a partner, take turns describing each of the four suspects. (Hair? Height? Weight? Clothing?) Then decide which man probably stole the purse. Use your subject description form.

SUSPECT   A   B   C   D

Choking is a common emergency. Listen to the following instructions; they tell how to help someone who is choking. Circle (a) or (b) to match each instruction with the correct picture.

Using the correct pictures, tell the steps to two classmates. Ask them to follow your directions. Then change roles.

PART five
Speaking Activities

activity **1**

Giving Advice. Look at pictures 1 to 6 below and on page 66. Each picture shows a person doing something dangerous. Notice the words under each picture. Work with a partner. Take turns looking at the pictures and words. Tell what not to do and explain why. Use may, could, or might to explain why. Use the words under the pictures to help you make sentences.

example: Don't jump over the net when you are playing tennis. You might get hurt.

1.

jump over the net / play tennis / get hurt

2.

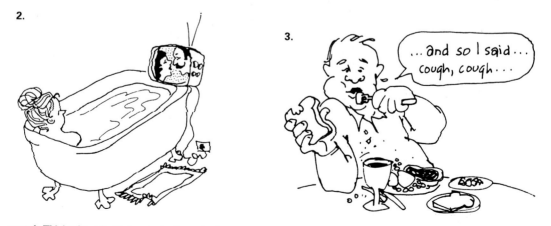

watch TV / take a bath / get electrocuted

3.

talk / eat food / choke

4.

smoke / lie in bed / start a fire

5.

drink beer / drive a car / have an accident

6.

leave your bag open / ride the bus / get robbed

 **Describing Emergencies.** Tell a group of classmates about an actual emergency or dangerous situation. Use the past continuous tense when possible.

> example: Last week I saw a fire. A big hotel was burning. Everyone was screaming.

 **Reporting an Emergency.** Work in pairs.

To Student A: You are watching an emergency situation. Call 911 to tell an emergency service operator what you see. Use the pictures above to help start a description, and then continue, using your imagination.

To Student B: Your job is to receive emergency phone calls. Ask questions to get necessary information about the emergency. Give useful instructions or suggestions to the caller if you can. The questions below will help you get started. Then use your imagination.

STUDENT B

1 { Questions: Address? Injury? What floor? Caller's location?
Instructions (what to do while waiting for help):

2 { Questions: Address? Injury? Caller's name? What are they doing?
Instructions:

3 { Questions: Location? Cars? Number of robbers? Injuries?
Instructions:

4 { Questions: What's wrong with child? Number of pills taken? Age? Address?
Kind of pills?
Instructions:

 **Evaluating Instructions.**   Discuss student B's instructions. Did he or she give good advice for each situation? What is the best thing to do in each situation? Your teacher may help you with this.

Role Play. Teresa's sister, Judy, is about to have a baby. The two women are driving to the hospital. On the way they have a flat tire. Can Teresa fix it? Is there enough time? What will they do?

Have your teacher explain the useful words and expressions below. Then prepare a conversation with a partner, and put on a skit about the situation.

The following words and phrases may help you express your ideas.

NOUNS	VERBS	
spare tire	to stop the car	to give a ride
tools	to be expecting	to get a ride
mechanic	to change a tire	to tow a car
tow truck	to be in labor	to have a baby

CHAPTER seven

Health

Useful Words and Expressions You will hear the following words and expressions in this chapter. If you are not sure what they mean, try to guess the meanings from the context.

to show (someone) around	sugar-free
to be in good shape	on a diet
to get in shape	Ouch!
a sore throat	a good workout
to take care of yourself	a health food store
to get better	a checkup
low-fat	

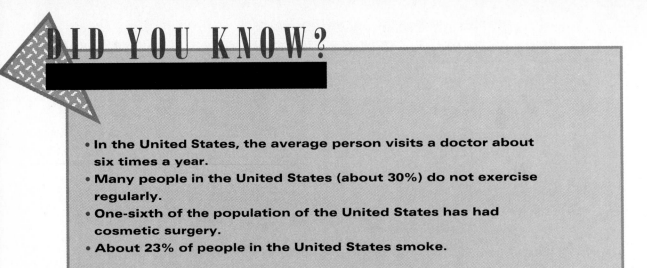

DID YOU KNOW?

- In the United States, the average person visits a doctor about six times a year.
- Many people in the United States (about 30%) do not exercise regularly.
- One-sixth of the population of the United States has had cosmetic surgery.
- About 23% of people in the United States smoke.

PART one
Listening to Conversations

prelistening questions

1. What do you do to try to stay healthy?
2. Do you have any habits that are bad for your health?

Getting the Main Idea

exercise 1

Peter and Kenji want to get in shape. They are thinking about joining a health club. Close your book and listen to their conversation. You may not understand every word. Listen for the main ideas.

exercise 2 Now you will hear seven questions about the conversation. Listen to the questions. Then write answers to the questions on the lines below. Discuss your answers with your classmates.

1. _____

2. _____

3. _____

4. _____

5. _____

6. _____

7. _____

Stress

exercise 3 Listen to the first part of the conversation again. Repeat each sentence during the pause. Then fill in the missing stressed words.

aerobics	harder	really
around	heart	show (*two times*)
beginners	here	think (*two times*)
do	instructors	use
good	like	week
great	looks	weight

INSTRUCTOR: I _____ you're going to _____ it here. Let me

_____ you _____ . Here's the _____

room. Our _____ can _____ you how to

_____ these machines.

PETER: That looks _____ , doesn't it?

KENJI: Yeah.

INSTRUCTOR: And _____ is our _____ class . . .

KENJI: Is this class for _____ ?

INSTRUCTOR: Well, it _____ like it, doesn't it? It's called "low impact,"

but they're _____ working _____ than you

_____ .

PETER: So that's pretty _____ for your _____ . . .

INSTRUCTOR: It sure is. But you should _____ it at least three times a

_____ if you want to be in good shape.

 **exercise 4**

Now listen to the rest of the conversation. Mark the stressed words.

KENJI: There are better ways to get in shape, aren't there?

INSTRUCTOR: Well, some people prefer swimming. Let me show you our pool . . .

PETER: Wow! Look at that woman in the middle lane. She's really fast!

INSTRUCTOR: Oh, yeah. That's Ellen, one of our instructors.

KENJI: I'd like to take lessons from *her*!

INSTRUCTOR: You're not the only one. C'mon, I'll show you the showers and the locker room. You know, you ought to join the club before the end of the month.

KENJI: Really? Why?

INSTRUCTOR: Because we have a special discount for students this month. Let's go to my office. I'll tell you all about it.

Intonation with Tag Questions

Questions at the end of sentences are called tag questions. Affirmative statements take negative tag questions: He is strong, isn't he? Negative statements take affirmative tag questions: She isn't tired, is she? People use tag questions in two ways. Listen to the following examples. Notice the difference in intonation.

1. Your father is a doctor, isn't he?↑
2. Your father is a doctor, isn't he?↓

In the first example, the speaker is unsure of the answer. His voice goes up: Your father is a doctor, isn't he?↑ In the second example, the speaker is almost sure the father is a doctor. His voice goes down: Your father is a doctor, isn't he?↓

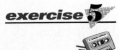 **exercise 5**

1. Repeat the first five sentences on the tape. As in the first example, the voice goes up at the end of the tag question.
2. Now repeat the next five sentences. As in the second example, the voice goes down at the end of the tag question.

exercise 6

Now listen to the examples from the dialogue. From the intonation, decide if the speaker was sure or unsure of the answer. Circle the correct answer.

1. sure   unsure
2. sure   unsure
3. sure   unsure
4. sure   unsure

PART two
Summarizing Main Ideas

exercise 1

Barbara is at the university health service. Listen to her conversation with her doctor.

exercise 2

Listen to the conversation again and take notes. The first one is done as an example.

BARBARA'S COMPLAINTS	DOCTOR'S ADVICE
1. terrible headache	1. eat right and get enough sleep
2. Stomach was upset	2. take 2 Aspirin two times a day
3. I'm feeling really weak	3. drink a lot of juice
4. my whole body feels hot	4. Gent plenty of rest
5. my muscles hurt	don't work too hard
6. Starting to get a sore throat	take care of yourself
7. I'm very tired	

exercise 3

Now use past-tense verbs to summarize Barbara's visit to the doctor. Include all the important information.

example: Barbara went to the doctor because she woke up with a terrible headache. She told the doctor that her stomach was upset.

PART three
Guessing Information

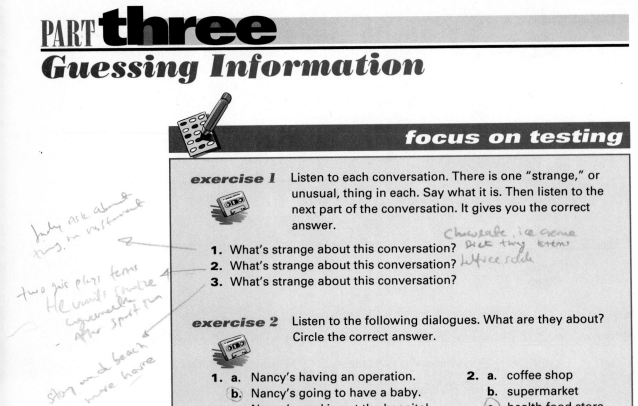

focus on testing

exercise 1 Listen to each conversation. There is one "strange," or unusual, thing in each. Say what it is. Then listen to the next part of the conversation. It gives you the correct answer.

1. What's strange about this conversation?
2. What's strange about this conversation?
3. What's strange about this conversation?

Handwritten notes (margins):
lady ask about thing in restaurant
two girls plays tennis
He want smoke cigarette after sport run
story and beach one more have
Chocolate, ice cream Diet thing items
biffee rddle

exercise 2 Listen to the following dialogues. What are they about? Circle the correct answer.

1. a. Nancy's having an operation.
   b. Nancy's going to have a baby.
   c. Nancy's working at the hospital

2. a. coffee shop
   b. supermarket
   c. health food store

THE NEW YORK TIMES, MONDAY, JUNE 6, 1994

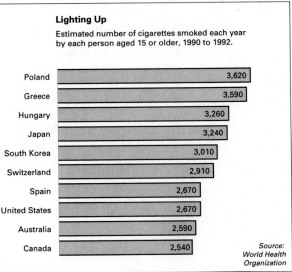

Lighting Up

Estimated number of cigarettes smoked each year by each person aged 15 or older, 1990 to 1992.

Poland	3,620
Greece	3,590
Hungary	3,260
Japan	3,240
South Korea	3,010
Switzerland	2,910
Spain	2,670
United States	2,670
Australia	2,590
Canada	2,540

Source: World Health Organization

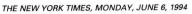

activity

You will hear three telephone conversations about health situations. Take notes on each call.

CONVERSATION 1

Reason for call: _for checkup._

Name of dentist: _Dr Jones_

Location: _Universal Dental Clinic_

Time of appointment: _around two o'clock_

CONVERSATION 2

Reason for call: _to know if her prescription is ready_

Name of patient: _Ellen Beattie_

Price of medicine: _$14.95_

Special instructions: _take the pills every six hours   Don't mix with alcohol_

Closing time: _until 5 o'clock_

CONVERSATION 3

First reason for call: _Change d'appointment with doctor Stave_

Name of baby's doctor: _Dr Stork_

Time of baby's new appointment: _ten o'clock_

Second reason for call: _Check up for her husband_

Time of husband's appointment: _6 o'clock_

Name of husband's doctor: _Dr Miller._

PART five

Speaking Activities

activity **1** **Giving Advice.** Working with a partner, describe the problem in each picture. Then match each picture with the correct remedy. Use *should, ought to,* or *had better* to make complete sentences.

example: He has a headache;
he should take some aspirin.

POSSIBLE REMEDIES

1. Drink tea.	**5.**	Bandage it.
2. Drink hot milk.	**6.**	Put ice on it.
3. Put it in hot water.	**7.**	Take some aspirin.
4. Take a cold shower.	**8.**	Take a sleeping pill.

1.

2.

3.

5.

4.

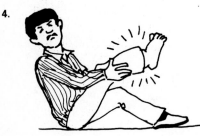

 **Comparing Popular Cures.** Tell the class about popular cures for common illnesses—things that a doctor wouldn't necessarily tell you to do.

> **examples:** My grandmother thinks that chicken soup is good for a cold.
> In my country we eat honey to cure a cough.

 **Talking About Heath.** Create a dialogue with a partner for one of the following situations. You can use the conversations in Part Four, page 75, as models.

SITUATION 1: Call your dentist to change an appointment. Include this information: (a) time of old appointment, (b) reason for change, (c) time of new appointment.

SITUATION 2: Make an appointment with a doctor. Include this information: (a) reason for call, (b) day you want to go in, (c) hours when the doctor can see you, (d) location of doctor's office, (e) what kind of insurance you have.

SITUATION 3: Tell your doctor about a health problem. Include this information: (a) your symptoms, (b) when they started, (c) how often you have them, (d) doctor's orders.

EXAMPLES OF SYMPTOMS

I have a $\begin{cases} \text{cough.} \\ \text{fever.} \\ \text{sore throat.} \end{cases}$

My arm hurts.

My (foot) is $\begin{cases} \text{sore.} \\ \text{swollen.} \end{cases}$

I feel $\begin{cases} \text{dizzy.} \\ \text{nauseous.} \end{cases}$

Culture Note

A psychologist is an adviser or a counselor who helps people with their personal problems. People from other cultures sometimes think that only "crazy people" visit psychologists. However, in North America many people feel comfortable getting advice from professionals who are specially trained to help them.

Role Play. Dr. Straithead, a psychologist, has many interesting patients. One of them is Mr. Robert Rich. He comes to Dr. Straithead's office every Wednesday to talk about his very unusual problem: He recently became a millionaire, but his family is worried because he is gambling a lot of his money away. They think he needs counseling.

Prepare a conversation with a partner, taking the roles of Dr. Straithead and Mr. Rich or one of Dr. Straithead's other patients:

- Jessica Bashful (who is very shy at parties and at work)
- Patrick D. Playboy (who cannot stay with just one girlfriend)
- Helen Hater (who is jealous of her very successful sister)

The following phrases may help you express your ideas.

I can't help it.	I advise you to. . . .
Why don't you. . . .	I suggest that you. . . .
You should. . . .	I want you to. . . .
You ought to. . . .	Try to. . . .
You had better. . . .	

CHAPTER eight

Entertainment and the Media

in this chapter

Useful Words and Expressions You will hear the following words and expressions in this chapter. If you are not sure what they mean, try to guess the meanings from the context.

That's my point.
I see what you mean.
to turn into (someone or something)
the news
to drive off the road
the top story
I guess
to hit the brakes
to run out of gas(oline)
to check it out
What's on (TV)?
game shows
western(s)
a comedy series

DID YOU KNOW?

- **Television viewers in the United States see, on average, 1 murder every 78 minutes.**
- **Male adults are twice as likely as women to make the decision about what the family will watch on TV.**
- **Ninety-five percent of people over 12 years of age in the United States listen to the radio for over 3 hours every work-day.**

PART one
Listening to Conversations

prelistening questions

1. How many hours of TV do you and family members watch each week?
2. How do you usually get information about what's happening in the world?

Getting the Main Idea

 *exercise 1*

Barbara and Marsha are talking about television and newspapers. They don't exactly agree. Close your book and listen to their conversation. You may not understand every word. Listen for the main ideas.

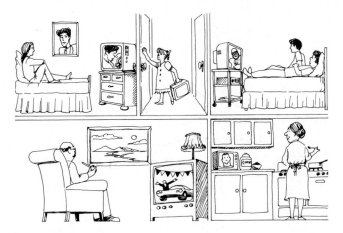

exercise 2

Now you will hear six questions about the conversation. Listen to the questions. Then write answers to the questions on the lines below. Discuss your answers with your classmates.

1. *They watch 6 hours tv a day*
2. *Because most programs are terrible*
3. *Some programs are bad a lot are ok.*
4. *She hate Comraical and she think News to never Talk too much*
5. *in the news paper she think they give more Information.*
6. *She found article*

Stress

exercise 3

Listen to the first part of the conversation again. Repeat each sentence during the pause. Then fill in the missing stressed words.

sports	programs	day	not	terrible
don't	news (*two times*)	right	family	joking
point	watch	hate	guess	tell
here	this	American	six	

BARBARA: Hey, listen to ____*this*____ ! The average ___*American*___

___*family*___ watches ____*six*____ hours of TV a day.

MARSHA: A ____*day*____ ! You're ____*joking*____ .

BARBARA: No, it says so ____*right*____ ____*here*____ in this magazine.

MARSHA: I ____*guess*____ I'm ____*watch*____ an average American. I usually

____*don't*____ ____*watch*____ TV at all. Most of the

____*Programs*____ are ____*terrible*____ .

BARBARA: Well, some of the programs are bad, but a lot are okay. And what about

the ____*Sport*____ and ____*news*____ ?

MARSHA: Well, yeah, I guess sports programs are okay. But for *a lot of* ,

I prefer a good newspaper.

BARBARA: Why do you say that?

MARSHA: Well, I ____*hate*____ all those commercials, and then the TV news

stories never ____*tell*____ you very much. A newspaper has more

information, and you can read just what you want to.

BARBARA: Yeah, I see what you mean.

exercise 4

Now listen to the rest of the conversation. Take notes, writing down key words (which are usually the stressed words) as in the following examples. Don't try to copy whole sentences. Then re-create the conversation with a partner, using your notes as a guide.

MARSHA: look at this _____

BARBARA: What? _____

MARSHA: article, TV, mystery, interesting _____

BARBARA: _____

MARSHA: _____

BARBARA: _____

PART **two**
Summarizing Main Ideas

exercise 1

You are going to hear a news report about an emergency situation. Predict what kind of information you might hear.

_____

_____

_____

exercise 2

Now listen to the report and check your predictions.

exercise 3

Listen to the news report again and take notes.

Location of plane: _Highway one_____

Number of passengers: _six_____

Number of passengers injured: _three four_____

Types of injuries: _Broke legs, Back injuries_____

Number of injured on the ground: _Nobody, none_____

Possible cause of emergency: _gaseline_____

exercise 4   Now work with a partner. Give a summary of the news report using the notes you just made.

PART **three**
Guessing Information

focus on testing

Listen to the following commercials. Circle the letter of the product being advertised in each one. Then listen to the next part of the commercial. It contains the correct answer.

1. a. soup
    b. breakfast cereal
    c. vitamins

2. a. bank
    b. sleeping pill
    c. telephone company

3. a. baby products
    b. a used car
    c. a new car

4. a. breakfast food
    b. TV magazine
    c. sleep aid

5. a. a magazine
    b. a daytime TV drama
    c. a news program

"Would you please pick something and quit channel surfing."

Drawing by Frascino; © 1979. The New Yorker Magazine, Inc.

activity 1

Marsha and her boyfriend want to watch TV tonight. First look at the section from their TV guide. Then answer the questions below.

TV TODAY		
WEDNESDAY		
7:30	**2** TWO ON THE TOWN Beauty advice; fashion show	
	4 _____ name of program	game show/musical/news
	7 EYE ON THE CITY A report on crime; a look at baby monkeys	
8 PM	**13** _____ name of program	movie/sports/game show/musical
	4 6 REAL PEOPLE Reports on a talking cow; bicycle racing; interview with recovering alcoholic	
	3 _____ name of program	western movie/comedy/sports
	☐ _____ name of program	movie/ interview/sports
	11 _____ name of program	game show/sports news
8:30	☐ NEWS	
	4 NEWS	
	9 NEWS	
9:00	☐ _____ name of program	sports/comedy series/news

1. What can they watch on Channel 2 at 7:30? _____

2. What time is the news on? _____

3. On what channels? _____

activity 2

Now listen to their conversation. Each time you hear a pause, fill in the missing information. Go over your answers with a group of classmates.

PART five
Speaking Activities

 **Describing TV Shows.**   Tell a partner about a TV show you like to watch. Use this space to organize your ideas.

example: I like to watch "Saturday Night Live." It's a comedy show with many different actors. The actors play different characters and perform funny skits. They perform before a live audience. There is a different guest host each week. The host is usually a famous actor or musician. There is also a special musical guest or group each week. I like the show because it is funny, and it has good music.

1. Kind of show (police story, comedy, mystery, talk show, etc.): _____

_____

2. Type of people in it (crazy detective, single mother, etc.): _____

_____

3. Situation (city police station, small-town coffee shop, etc.):_____

_____

4. Reasons you like it (funny, exciting, educational, etc.):_____

_____

 **Describing Movies.**   Try to tell your partner the story of a movie you like. Tell only the most important parts.

activity 3 **Comparing TV Programs.**   How are TV programs different in your home country from those in the United States or Canada? How are they similar? Discuss these questions in small groups.

Discussing Censorship. *Censorship* is the restriction or prohibition of words or images in the media. People in power decide what is acceptable (or unacceptable) to watch, listen to, or read based on political, religious, or moral beliefs. Sex, violence, and "swear words" are typical areas for censorship.

How do you feel about censorship? In what situations is it right, or wrong? Discuss this issue in small groups. The following expressions may help you express your ideas.

TO AGREE	TO DISAGREE
I agree.	I disagree.
I think so, too.	I don't think so.
That's what I think.	I don't believe that.
I'm sure that's true.	I'm not sure that's true.
That's true.	That's not true.
You're right.	You're wrong.
I feel the same way.	I don't feel the same way.

Role Play. Isabella and her husband often fight about TV programs. She prefers to watch cultural shows with dance or music, but her husband likes to watch news and business reports. Unfortunately, they only have one TV set.

Prepare a conversation about this situation with a partner. Use ideas and vocabulary you have learned in this chapter. Then put on a skit about the situation. The following phrases may help you express your ideas.

REQUESTS

Could we
Why don't we } watch the (news)?
Do you mind if we

How about watching the (ballet)?

POSSIBLE RESPONSES

AGREE	REFUSE
Sure.	No way.
Why not?	Not a chance.
O.K.	I don't want to.
Well, all right.	Let's watch the (ballet).
I guess so.	I'd rather watch the (the news).

CHAPTER **nine**

Social Life

in this chapter

Useful Words and Expressions You will hear the following words and expressions in this chapter. If you are not sure what they mean, try to guess the meanings from the context.

What have you been up to?   a pain in the neck
No kidding!   live music
No way!   cover charge
Come on!   a date
a blind date   you guys
in ages

DID YOU KNOW?

- In many parts of the United States, high school students celebrate their upcoming graduation at a "prom." To attend this formal dance, couples often spend hundreds of dollars on tickets, clothing, flowers, and a chauffeur-driven limousine.
- In San Francisco, there are unofficial "singles nights" at some local supermarkets. On these evenings, unmarried men and women gather for the purpose of meeting potential dates while they are doing their food shopping.
- In the 1990s, about half of all couples who get married in the United States live together before marriage.

PART **one**
Listening to Conversations

prelistening questions

1. Have you ever had a reunion with old friends? What did you talk about?
2. Has your social life changed in the last few years? Do you have more or fewer friends?
3. Do you go out more or less frequently? Why?

Getting the Main Idea

exercise 1

Herb is visiting his hometown in Texas. He meets two old friends on the street. Close your book and listen to their conversation. You may not understand every word. Listen for the main ideas.

Interactions I • Listening/Speaking

exercise 2

Now you will hear five questions about the conversation. Listen to the questions. Then write answers to the questions on the lines below. Discuss your answers with your classmates.

1. _Many year ago._
2. _Is great._
3. _She gut new job the sally computer_
4. _because she tra-ailing over the country_
5. _she was porally surprise because Yolanda is married with Carl walters_

Stress

exercise 3

Listen to the first part of the conversation again. Repeat each sentence during the pause. Then fill in the missing stressed words.

studying	great (*two times*)	believe
know	lots	hard
up (*two times*)	computer	major
science	you	are
sure	can't	ages

SALLY: Yolanda, I ___Can't___ ___belive___ it! Look! It's Herb

Myers. How ___are___ you?

HERB: Sally? Yolanda? Wow! I haven't seen you guys in ___ages___ !

YOLANDA: I ___Know___ . You look ___great___ !

HERB: Thanks! You too.

YOLANDA: So what have you been ___up___ to?

HERB: ___lots___ of things. I'm at Faber College now.

SALLY: Really? That's ___great___ !

HERB: Yeah, I've been ___studying___ pretty ___hard___ so far.

YOLANDA: ___Sure___ you have . . .

SALLY: What's your ___major___ — tennis?

HERB: No, it's . . . uh . . . actually, ___Computer___ ___science___ . Anyway, what have ___you___ guys been ___up___ to all year?

exercise 4

Now listen to the rest of the conversation. Take notes, writing down key words as in the example. Don't try to copy whole sentences. Then re-create the conversation with a partner, using your notes as a guide.

YOLANDA: *Got married, baby boy* _____

HERB: _____

SALLY: _____

_____

HERB: _____

_____

YOLANDA: _____

Intonation with Exclamations

To express strong feelings (surprise, anger, happiness), we use exclamations. These are expressions that we pronounce with especially strong emphasis and with falling intonation at the end.

examples: Wow! I can't believe it! That's great! That's awful!

 **exercise 5**

Repeat the following exclamations from the dialogue. Follow the stress and intonation patterns carefully.

Yolanda! I can't believe it!
Look!
Wow! I haven't seen you
  guys in ages!
You look great!
That's great!
No kidding!
Congratulations!
No way!
That's terrific!

exercise 6

Now listen to some statements and questions on the tape. During the pause, respond with an exclamation. Use a different exclamation each time.

example: *You hear:* I just got six hundred on my TOEFL test.
          You say: That's great!

You will hear six speakers.

PART two
Summarizing Main Ideas

exercise 1 Listen as Sally tries to arrange a "blind date" for her friend Beverly. A blind date is an arranged date between two people who don't know each other.

exercise 2 Listen again and take notes about Franco.

   Appearance: _____

   Job: _____

   Interests: _____

   Age: _____

   Drawbacks: _____

exercise 3 Describe Franco to a partner. Use your notes from Exercise 2 to help you.

exercise 4 You'll hear a brief lecture on American football. What do you know about this sport? Have you ever seen an American football game? What do the players look like? As you listen, you might try to compare it to football or soccer in your home country.

exercise 5 Listen to the talk again and take notes.

   Football season: _____

   Kinds of teams: _____

   Uniforms (clothing): _____

   Object (goal) of game: _____

   "Pro" (professional) players: _____

   Games on TV: _____

exercise 6 Describe American football to a partner, using your notes from Exercise 5.

PART three
Guessing Information

Listen to the following conversations from Larry's party. Circle the sentence that best describes each conversation. Then listen to the next part. It gives you the correct answer.

1. a. The man doesn't like the town.
    b. The man recently came to the town.
    c. The woman doesn't know the town very well.

2. a. The manager hurt his neck.
    b. The man works with the woman.
    c. The man and the woman used to work together.

3. a. The man likes to spend a lot of money.
    b. The woman doesn't really want to go out with the man.
    c. The woman likes the man very much.

4. a. The man is very worried about Tony.
    b. There are four kinds of Scotch at the party.
    c. The woman thinks Tony has been drinking too much.

5. a. The man and the woman will leave the party in forty-five minutes.
    b. The man and the woman are angry because of a misunderstanding.
    c. The woman drove the man to the party.

PART four
Listening Tasks

activity

Sally and Herb plan to go out over the weekend. Sally's making a few telephone calls to get some information. Think about what kind of information she needs from (1) a movie theater, (2) a nightclub, and (3) a friend giving a party. Listen to each call and take notes.

1. Name of movie theater: _FOX_

Location of movie theater: _Town and Country_
Shopping Center

Name of movie: _Love Affair_

Show times: _for Saturday are two, six an ten o'clock_

Price of tickets: _$ 8.00, $4.50 for students_

Telephone number for more information: _5550832_

2. Name of nightclub: _Terry's Jazz Club_

Entertainment: _Brazilian singer_

Cost: _10 cover charge but dinner is free the show_

Menu: _Specialty Italian food, but we served salads and Hamburgers_

Reservations: _two_   _eight_   _friday night at eight_
     Number of people   Time   Date

3. Name of person giving party: _Larry_

Address: _825 Spring Street_

Location: _Three Blocks west of the town and country Shopping center_

Time: _Any time after eight_

What to bring: _Some beer or wine._

PART five
Speaking Activities

activity 1 **Discussing Social Customs.**   Discuss with your classmates the following questions about social customs as they apply to your home country and to North America. Ask your teacher about U.S. and Canadian customs if you're not sure.

1. Who pays
   a. if a man and a woman are on a date?
   b. if friends go out to dinner?

2. Is it all right to be half an hour late if you're invited to . . .
   a. dinner at someone's house?
   b. lunch at a restaurant?
   c. a party?

3. What kind of gift should you bring
   a. to a dinner party?
   b. for a friend's birthday?
   c. to a sick friend?

4. What do you do if you cannot accept an invitation?
   a. Say "Yes" but don't go.
   b. Say "Thank you" and explain why you can't go.
   c. Say "Maybe" even if you're sure you won't go.

5. What do you do if someone offers you a food you don't like?
   a. Eat it anyway and say nothing.
   b. Tell the truth.
   c. Make a polite excuse such as "Thanks, but I'm full."

activity 2 **Finding a Spouse.**   Get in groups of three or four and discuss the following questions. In your home country, how do people find husbands and wives? Do they meet each other through family introductions, through professional matchmakers, in school, at work, or in some other way?

Individually survey two or three married Americans to find out how and where they met their spouses. Report the results to your group. How does the way Americans find husbands and wives compare to the ways people do this in your home country?

activity 3 **Calling for Information.**   Look in your local newspaper's entertainment section.

1. Choose three activities. For example, you might decide on a movie, sporting event, or dinner at a restaurant.
2. Call to get the information you need for each activity. Ask about cost, schedule, travel directions, etc.
3. Report the information to the class.

To prepare for this activity, review the telephone conversations in Part Four, page 93.

Compliments. In the United States and Canada, compliments are common and accepted. People give compliments to make other people feel comfortable, to be friendly, or simply to start conversations.

> **examples:** Maria, your English is really improving.
> Excuse me. Who cut your hair? I really like it.
> You really have a beautiful home, Mrs. Johnson.

To accept compliments, the common answer is "Thanks." Sometimes we answer one compliment with another.

> **example:** A: You look great, Marge.
> B: Thanks. So do you, Bob.

In small groups, practice giving and accepting compliments. Here are some possible topics:

1. an item of clothing
2. a hair style
3. something someone did
4. a change someone made recently

Role Play. Many people think that a dating service is a good place to find a partner. Rose, for example, is a businesswoman and doesn't have time to look for a boyfriend. Richard, a divorced teacher, doesn't want to make a mistake again; he wants to choose the "right" woman this time. Can a video dating service help them?

Take the role of Rose or Richard as they make a video for the dating service. Give a short presentation in which you describe yourself and the person you're looking for (or you can be yourself and use your own information). Look at the dating service application form on the next page to get ideas. If you have video equipment, videotape your presentation.

The following expressions may help you express your ideas.

> I prefer. . . .   I can't stand. . . .
> I'd rather. . . .   I really dislike. . . .
> I love. . . .   I don't care for. . . .
> It's absolutely necessary that. . . .   I'm not interested in. . . .
> It doesn't matter if. . . .
> I don't care if. . . .

Name _____ Age _____ Male ☐ Female ☐

Address _____ Occupation: _____

_____ Work hours _____ Work Phone _____

THE PERSON I AM LOOKING FOR:

Age   from ☐   to ☐

Education   high school ☐ 2-year school ☐ some college ☐ college degree ☐

Occupation   clerical ☐ technical ☐ managerial ☐ professional ☐

Marital status   never married ☐ divorced ☐ widowed ☐ doesn't matter ☐

Interests   sports ☐ music ☐ movies ☐ dancing ☐ nature ☐

ABOUT MYSELF:

*Situation
new in town ☐
very busy ☐
shy ☐
interested in marriage ☐

*Marital status
never married ☐
divorced ☐
widowed ☐

*Plans
not planning to move ☐
planning to move soon ☐

*Interests
sports ☐
music ☐
movies ☐
dancing ☐
nature ☐

*Children
have ☐
don't have ☐
want ☐
doesn't matter ☐

After all the presentations, try to choose the "right" partner for each of your classmates.

CHAPTER ten

Customs, Celebrations, and Holidays

Useful Words and Expressions You will hear the following words and expressions in this chapter. If you are not sure what they mean, try to guess the meanings from the context.

a picnic   the bride   a honeymoon
fireworks   the groom   a surprise party
Trick or treat!

in this chapter

DID YOU KNOW?

- People in the United States spend over $7.4 billion a year on greeting cards.
- On July 4, 1991, 75,000 people attended a party celebrating the 115th birthday of Canada and the 215th birthday of the United States, making it the largest birthday party in history.
- Thelma Lucas was 84 and Harry Stevens was 103 when they were married on December 3, 1984, in Wisconsin, making them the oldest bride and groom on record.

PART**one**
Listening to Conversations

prelistening questions

1. Do people celebrate a romantic holiday like Valentine's Day in your home country? If so, how is it celebrated?
2. When do people customarily give gifts in your country?

Getting the Main Idea

exercise 1

Kenji is dating an American girl he met in class. He wants to buy her a gift for Valentine's Day to show her that he really likes her. Close your book and listen to the conversation between Kenji and the gift shop clerk. You may not understand every word. Listen for the main ideas.

98

exercise 2

Now you will hear five questions about the conversation. Listen to the questions. Then write answers to the questions on the lines below. Discuss your answers with your classmates.

1. _____

2. _____

3. _____

4. _____

5. _____

Stress

 **exercise 3**

Listen to the first part of the conversation again. Repeat each sentence during the pause. Then fill in the missing stressed words.

chocolate	girlfriend	giving
Valentine's	diet	get
her	too	
what	jewelry	

CLERK: Yes, can I help you with anything?

KENJI: I'm looking for a _____ gift for my _____ . Well, actually she's not my girlfriend yet, so I really don't know _____

to _____ her.

CLERK: How about some _____ ?

KENJI: Well, I think she's on a _____ .

CLERK: Hmm, then how about some _____ ?

KENJI: Gosh, I can't really spend _____ much money.

 **exercise 4**

Now listen to the rest of the conversation. Take notes, writing down key words as in the example. Don't try to copy whole sentences. Then re-create the conversation with a partner, using your notes as a guide.

CLERK: *bottle of cologne, she'll like that* _____

KENJI: _____

CLERK: _____

KENJI: _____

CLERK: _____

KENJI: _____

PART two

Summarizing Main Ideas

 **exercise 1**   You are going to hear a conversation about Thanksgiving, which is a truly American holiday. Before listening to it, predict some of the vocabulary or kinds of information you might hear.

_____

_____

_____

 **exercise 2**   Now listen to the conversation, checking your predictions and trying to learn more about the holiday.

 **exercise 3**   Listen to the conversation again and take notes.

Description of first Thanksgiving: _____

_____

_____

Reason for holiday: _____

_____

When celebrated: _____

Foods eaten: _____

_____

 **exercise 4**   Check your notes with a partner. Then close your books and practice telling each other how, when, and why Americans celebrate Thanksgiving.

PART three
Guessing Information

Listen to the following conversations about holidays and celebrations. Decide what each situation is. Circle the best answer in your book. Then listen to the next part of the conversation. It contains the correct answer.

1. a. the president's birthday
   b. the Fourth of July
   c. New Year's Eve

2. a. Christmas
   b. Thanksgiving
   c. Halloween

3. a. Christmas
   b. the man's birthday
   c. Valentine's Day

4. a. New Year's Day
   b. Christmas
   c. a birthday

5. a. a wedding
   b. a party
   c. a birthday party

PART four
Listening Tasks

Peter, Barbara, Herb, and Kenji are planning a surprise birthday party for Mike.

 **activity 1**

With a partner, make a short list of things you would need to do to give a birthday party.

_____

_____

 **activity 2**

Now listen to the conversation. Are Mike's friends planning to do the same things that are on your list? What are they planning that's *not* on your list?

_____

_____

activity 3

Listen again. What will each person do to prepare for the party? Briefly describe each job you hear next to the name of the person who agrees to do it.

Peter _____

Barbara _____

Kenji _____

Herb _____

PART five
Speaking Activities

activity 1

What's Wrong?   Working in small groups, take turns explaining what is wrong with each of these drawings.

example: You don't put jack-o'-lanterns under a Christmas tree.

1.

2.

3.

 **Describing Holidays.**   Now describe to a partner some major holidays in your country. How do people celebrate each one?

 **Using Gerunds and Infinitives.**   Think about a past holiday or vacation and then tell a partner about it. Use *be interested in, enjoy, spend* plus a gerund (*-ing* word) to make a number of sentences.

> **example:**   Last Christmas, I *spent* all morning *opening* gifts.

Now think about your next holiday or vacation. Use *need, plan, want, hope, would like* plus an infinitive (to + verb) to describe your plans to your partner.

> **example:**   Next summer, I *hope to visit* Yosemite National Park.

 **Invitations.**   Look at the following invitations here and on the next page. With a classmate, create a conversation for each invitation. One of you invites, and the other accepts (or politely refuses), and makes a related question or comment. After practicing with your partner, present a conversation to the class. Here are some expressions that are useful when accepting or refusing invitations.

TO INVITE	TO ACCEPT	TO REFUSE
Would you like to. . . ?	Yes, I'd love to . . .	I'd love to, but . . .
Do you want to. . . ?	I'd be delighted to . . .	I'm sorry but . . .
Why don't you (we). . . ?	That sounds great!	I wish I could, but . . .

Note: The blank spaces are to guide you, but remember that this is an oral, not a written, exercise.

> **example:**   A: Can you come over for dinner tonight?
>
> B: <u>Sure, I'd love to</u> . <u>What time?</u>
>
> A: <u>Around seven o'clock.</u>

A. I know about a Halloween party on Saturday. Do you want to go?

B. _____ . _____ ?

A. _____ .

A. What are you doing on New Year's Eve? Can you join us?

B. _____ . _____ ?

A. _____ .

A. There's a new movie at the Fox Theater. Do you want to go see it?

B. _____ . _____ ?

A. _____ .

Refusing Invitations.   With another classmate, *refuse* the following invitations. Give an excuse. To be polite, you should try to explain why you can't accept. You might suggest getting together another time. Here are some ways to refuse an invitation.

examples: Thanks, but I can't. I have to work.
Thanks for asking, but I have other plans.
I'd love to, but I'm busy. Maybe some other time.

A. Would you like to go skiing in Switzerland with me?

B. _____ .

A. Why don't you have a cup of coffee with us?

B. _____ .

A. Do you want to go to the ball game tomorrow? I have an extra ticket.

B. _____ .

A. We're going dancing Saturday night. Would you like to come?

B. _____ .

Role Play.   Today is Carol and David's wedding day. One hundred guests are waiting for them in the church. Everyone is very excited, except Carol. She is too nervous. In fact, she doesn't want to get married at all. She has only five minutes to tell David why she's changed her mind and doesn't want to marry him.

Based on the situation in the cartoon, prepare a conversation with a partner. Then put on a skit for the class. These expressions for expressing or reacting to bad news will be helpful.

EXPRESSING BAD NEWS	REACTING TO BAD NEWS
I've got some bad news. . . .	I'm speechless!
Please forgive me, but. . . .	I don't know what to say.
You'd better sit down. . . .	I can't believe it!
I don't know how to put this. . . .	Say it isn't so!
	That's fine with me.
	No problem.

CHAPTER eleven

Science and Technology

Useful Words and Expressions You will hear the following words and expressions in this chapter. If you are not sure what they mean, try to guess the meanings from the context.

pretty soon	get rotten
sounds creepy	top speed
are supposed to	recharge the batteries
mess around with	cut down on
the wave of the future	gadgets

DID YOU KNOW?

- **Eighty-five percent of all scientists who have ever lived are alive today.**
- **An estimated 26,000 scientific journal articles are published every day worldwide.**
- **In the United States, there is one computer for every 4 people. This compares with one for every 10 Germans, one for every 12 Japanese, and one for every 1,500 Chinese.**
- **Only 15 percent of Americans believe that advanced technological developments will have a big impact on their lives in the next 10 years.**

PART **ONE**
Listening to Conversations

prelistening questions

1. Look at the picture below. Where are the students?
2. What are they doing?
3. Have you ever done anything like that?

Getting the Main Idea

exercise 1

Peter, Herb, Kenji, and Kenji's new girlfriend, Lisa, are discussing which parts of Faber College's new museum of science and technology they want to visit first. Close your books and listen to their conversation. You may not understand every word. Listen for the main ideas.

exercise 2

Now you will hear five questions about the conversation. Listen to the questions. Then write answers to the questions on the lines below. Discuss your answers with your classmates.

1. _____

2. _____

3. _____

4. _____

5. _____

Stress

exercise 3

Now listen to the first part of the conversation again. Some of the stressed words are missing. Repeat each sentence during the pause. Then fill in the missing stressed words.

Japan	service	do	New York
where	skate	transportation	really
speeds (*two times*)	Germany	interesting	friction
magnets	video	safer	incredible
huge	start	miss	cool

PETER: So where should we _____ ? This place is _____ !

LISA: Why don't we check out the _____ exhibit?

KENJI: Right! I _____ want to see that Maglev train that

_____ along on air.

HERB: How do they _____ that?

LISA: Isn't it _____ that keep the train about a foot above the tracks?

KENJI: Uh huh. And there isn't any _____ , so the train can reach

_____ _____ .

PETER: I hear that _____ and _____ are going to have

Maglev trains in _____ pretty soon.

HERB: Sounds _____ . But let's not _____ the virtual reality

lab. It's really _____ . No matter _____ you are, you

just put on a _____ helmet and you can be in

_____ —walk the streets, _____ through Central

Park—and you never even leave the room!

KENJI: It's probably a lot _____ to see New York that way.

exercise 4

Now listen to the rest of the conversation. Take notes, writing down key words. Don't try to copy whole sentences. Then re-create the conversation with a partner, using your notes as a guide.

LISA: _____

PETER: _____

LISA: _____

PETER: _____

HERB: _____

PART **two**
Summarizing Main Ideas

exercise 1

You are going to hear someone talk about electric cars. Listen for the main ideas only. Use the space below to take notes.

_____

_____

_____

_____

_____

_____

_____

_____

_____

_____

_____

_____

_____

_____

_____

_____

exercise 2 Listen again, and organize your notes using the outline form below. Mention only the key advantages, disadvantages, and future of electric cars. Compare your finished outline with those of classmates. Then retell the story in your own words.

I. Advantages

    a. _____

    b. _____

II. Disadvantages

    a. _____

    b. _____

    c. _____

III. Future developments

    a. _____

    b. _____

    c. _____

PART three
Guessing Information

focus on testing

Listen to the following conversations about problems caused by machines. Decide what kinds of machines they are talking about. Circle your answers and then compare them with classmates and discuss the reasons for your choices.

1. a. oven
   b. air-conditioner
   c. thermometer

2. a. tape recorder
   b. lamp
   c. answering machine

3. a. photo copier
   b. car
   c. vacuum cleaner

4. a. cellular phone
   b. TV set
   c. CD player

5. a. camera
   b. photo copier
   c. fax machine

6. a. computer
   b. TV
   c. car

PART four
Listening Tasks

activity **1**

Peter has never learned how to set the clock on his VCR. Lisa has offered to show him how to set the clock. Before you listen to Lisa's explanation, work with a partner and discuss these questions.

1. Are there any machines that you find confusing or difficult to use? What are they?
2. What makes them difficult or confusing?
3. What machines are you good at using? How did you learn to use them?
4. Do you like to read instruction manuals? Why or why not?

activity **2**

Look at the illustration below as you listen to Lisa explain how to set a VCR clock. The picture shows the buttons on the VCR. Listen carefully to Lisa's instructions. For each step she describes, write the step number over the button or buttons Peter should push.

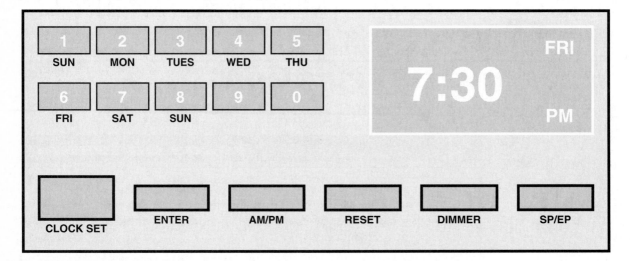

PART five
Speaking Activities

activity **1**

Cartoon. Talk about the cartoon Cathy on page 111 with a partner. What is the main idea it communicates? Do you agree or disagree? Why?

 **Electronic Items.** In groups of three or four, make lists of all the electronic gadgets and appliances you have in your home.

_____

_____

_____

_____

What would life be like if you had to live without these items?

> **example:** If I didn't have a VCR, I wouldn't be able to tape programs on TV. I also wouldn't be able to rent movies from the video store.

Then name five things not on your list that you would really like to have and explain why you want them.

> **example:** I'd really like to have a CD-ROM. I could get an encyclopedia on CD to find information faster.

activity 3

Giving Instructions. Describe to a partner how to operate a device such as a fax machine, automatic teller machine, photocopier, or coffee maker. You may want to draw simple pictures or diagrams as you talk. (Ask your teacher if you need help with vocabulary.) Use the expressions below to find out how much the other person has understood, and to show how much you have understood.

TO ASK IF SOMEONE UNDERSTOOD	TO CONFIRM UNDERSTANDING	TO SHOW LACK OF UNDERSTANDING
Did you get that?	Uh huh.	Wait. Could you repeat that?
Are you following me?	Got it.	I didn't get that.
Is this clear?	Gotcha (Got you.)	Could you go over that again?
Okay so far?	Yup.	I'm not following you.

activity 4

Role Play. A "technophobe" is a person who is afraid of new technology. Kevin is a technophobe. His wife, Tina, however, loves to buy electronic gadgets of all kinds. She usually has a hard time explaining to Kevin why they are necessary and how they work. Play the roles of Kevin and Tina and act out a conversation based on the cartoon below. If possible, use some of the expressions from Activity 3.

CHAPTER twelve

You, the Consumer

Useful Words and Expressions You will hear the following words and expressions in this chapter. If you are not sure what they mean, try to guess the meaning from the context

a car dealer	Yuk!
built in	to make an offer
remote control	to shoot (a picture)
Calm down!	dirt cheap
garage sale	ridiculous
a queen-size bed	under warranty
frost-free	to bargain
to test drive	

DID YOU KNOW?

- **Every day Americans buy at least 5 million objects with the image of Mickey Mouse on them.**
- **The West Edmonton Mall in Alberta, Canada, is the world's largest shopping center. It has 11 major department stores and 800 independent stores, and it serves over 500,000 shoppers a week.**
- **Citibank, the leading bank card company in the United States, has over 10 million credit card accounts.**

PART one
Listening to Conversations

prelistening questions

1. What kinds of things do you like shopping for, and in what type of stores do you look for them? (For example: skis; in a sporting goods store.)
2. How are salesclerks in your hometown or country different from those in other places you have visited or lived?
3. How do prices in your home country compare with prices in the United States (or other places you have visited or lived)?

Getting the Main Idea

exercise 1

Marsha is shopping in a large department store. Close your books and listen to this conversation between Marsha, a salesclerk, and another customer. You may not understand every word. Listen for the main ideas.

Now you will hear five questions about the conversation. Listen to the questions. Then write answers to the questions on the lines below. Discuss your answers with your classmates.

1. _____

2. _____

3. _____

4. _____

5. _____

Stress

Now listen to the first part of the conversation again. Some of the stressed words are missing. Repeat each sentence during the pause. Then fill in the missing stressed words.

terrific	easy	both	got
help (*two times*)	get	fifty	case
silk	striped	blue	
designer	there	right	
ties (*two times*)	first	I	

MAN: Miss! Could I please _____ some _____ here?

SALESWOMAN: Certainly, sir. I'll be _____ _____ .

MARSHA: I believe _____ was here _____ .

SALESWOMAN: All right. What can I _____ you with?

MARSHA: I'm interested in those _____ in that _____ .

MAN: I'd like to see those _____ . (both laugh)

SALESWOMAN: Well, that makes it _____ . Why don't you

_____ take a look at what we've _____ .

These are our _____ ties, and they're _____

dollars each.

MARSHA: Are they all _____ ?

SALESWOMAN: Uh-huh.

MAN: Oh, I think I like this _____ one in _____ .

MARSHA: Wow, that's really gorgeous. It would look _____ on

you.

exercise 4 Now listen to the rest of the conversation. Take notes, writing down key words. Don't try to copy whole sentences. Then re-create the conversation with a partner, using your notes as a guide.

MAN: _____

MARSHA: _____

_____

MAN: _____

SALESWOMAN: _____

MARSHA: _____

MAN: _____

_____

MARSHA: _____

_____

PART **two**
Summarizing Main Ideas

exercise 1  You are going to hear a radio show about how to buy a used car. Listen for the main ideas only. Use the space below to take notes.

_____

_____

_____

_____

_____

_____

_____

_____

_____

_____

_____

 **exercise 2**

Listen again, and organize your notes using the outline form below. Mention only the key ideas. Compare your finished outline to those of your classmates.

I. Introduction

_____

_____

II. Places to buy

A. _____

    1. Advantages:_____

    2. Disadvantages: _____

B. _____

    1. Advantages:_____

    2. Disadvantages: _____

    3. Questions to ask: _____

       _____

       _____

 **exercise 3**

Review your notes. Then close your book and work with a partner. Take turns summarizing what you have learned about buying a used car.

PART three
Guessing Information

In this section, you will hear six consumer complaints. After you listen to each one, listen to the announcer's question and circle the correct answer. Then listen to the next part of the tape. It contains the correct answer to the previous question.

1. a. a radio
    b. a battery
    c. a watch

2. a. his credit card
    b. his telephone bill
    c. his airline bill

3. a. spoiled milk
    b. rotten eggs
    c. spoiled meat

4. a. to the painter
    b. to the tailor
    c. to the hairdresser

5. a. The customer will probably find her receipt.
    b. The customer will probably get her money back.
    c. The customer will probably decide to exchange the gift.

6. a. for the repair work
    b. for the broken parts
    c. for the new TV set

PART four
Listening Tasks

activity 1

It's the end of the school year, and Peter and Kenji are renting an unfurnished apartment for the summer. They are interested in buying a few things, and they are calling people who advertised in the newspaper. Match each telephone conversation with the correct newspaper ad shown on page 119. Circle a, b, or c. As you listen, underline the clues that helped you choose the correct answer.

a.

1. Sears fridge—works like new. Great for apartments, dorms. Only $100, firm. Call 555-5313.

b.

White, bar-sized refrig. Brand new w/warranty. Must sell—$150 or best offer. Call eves: 555-2341.

c.

Family size refrig. Brown w/ ice maker. Excell. cond. Reasonably priced. Call Mary: 555-1111.

a.

2. Japanese mountain bike. Perfect shape—used only twice by pro racer. $275 o.b.o. Call 555-1910.

b.

Lady's mountain bike, 26-inch frame, new tires. Must sell—leaving country. Needs minor repair. Call 555-4988.

c.

Two great bikes! Men's mountain Schwinn, Lady's 10-speed Huffy. Each $300 new. Will sell CHEAP! Tel: 555-6789.

a.

3. New 20" RCA color TV— won on TV game show. $300. Call 555-2565.

b.

1990 RCA color console. New picture tube. Works like new. $200. Call 555-4567.

c.

Almost-new hotel TVs at great discount! 90-day guarantee. Call 555-5780.

a.

4. Garage sale. All my furniture must go: chairs, tables, couch, office desk, and much more. Come early Sat. A.M. for best selection. Tel: 555-9999.

b.

Modern Danish desk. All wood, great for office or home. $175. Call Saturday: 555-0000.

c.

Office furn. clearance! All desks must go—cheap. Filing cabinets 20% off. Call for prices 9–5: 555-4588.

activity 2

Look at the floor plan of the department store. It shows the location of the different departments on the second floor. You will hear people give directions to four departments. Listen to each person and follow the directions. Write the name of each department on the map.

Listen to the directions again. Then check your answers with a classmate.

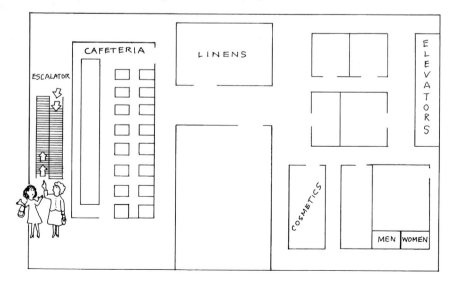

PART five
Speaking Tasks

Classified Ads. Collect some newspaper classified ads for things you might be interested in buying and bring them to class. Choose one of the ads and carefully prepare a list of the questions you might ask the seller. Then call the seller (or role play the call with the teacher or with another student). Use the expressions below to ask for or give information.

BUYER	SELLER
To Ask the Price	*To Describe the Price*
How much is it?	It's a fair price.
How much do you want?	It's a bargain.
	It's a steal.
To Try to Get a Lower Price	*To Hold the Price*
Is that as low as you'll go?	That's the best I can do.
Is that your best price?	The price is firm.
Will you take (five) dollars?	Take it or leave it.
How about (five) dollars?	
	To Invite a Lower Price
	I might take a little less.
	Make me an offer.
To Conclude	*To Conclude*
I'll take it.	So, what do you think?
Let me think about it.	What do you say?
Thanks anyway.	I'm sure you'll like it.

Buying Things. Play the roles of Peter or Kenji and the seller of the items in Part Four: Listening Tasks, pages 118 to 119. The buyer (Peter or Kenji) goes to the seller's home to try to buy each of the items. Use the expressions above and try to agree on a fair price.

Consumer Complaints. Work with a partner. Using situations and language similar to those presented in Part Three: Guessing Information, page 118, take turns playing the roles of a store employee and a customer complaining about something. Describe the problem and decide if you want an exchange, a refund, or a reduced charge. Use situations that have happened or might actually happen to you.

120

Interactions I • Listening/Speaking

 **Role Play.**   Andrea has always respected older people. One day she sees a woman old enough to be her grandmother shoplifting a pair of gloves in a department store. Should she talk to the elderly lady, call the manager, or what? Prepare a conversation with a partner showing what you and the woman might say to each other. Then prepare a second conversation showing what the woman might say to the store manager. Share your conversations with your classmates if you wish.

Tapescript

School Life

PART **one** *Listening to Conversations, page 2*

Getting the Main Idea

exercise 1

Jack, Peter, and Herb are new students at Faber College. They meet in the student lounge of their dormitory. Close your book and listen to their conversation. You may not understand every word. Listen for the main ideas.

JACK: Hi! How're you doing?
PETER: Oh, hi! You're Jack, right?
JACK: That's right. What's your name again?
PETER: Peter. Peter Riley.
JACK: Peter, this is my roommate, Herb.
PETER: Hi, Herb.
HERB: Nice to meet you.
PETER: Are you from Texas?
HERB: Yeah. Why? Do you think I have an accent?
PETER: Yeah.
HERB: Ha! You're the ones with the accent!
JACK: Listen, Peter. We're really hungry. Do you want to get something to eat with us?
PETER: I can't. I have to meet my new roommate.
HERB: Oh, yeah? Well, okay. Listen, stop by and see us. We're up in 212.
PETER: Hey, we're on the same floor. Room 220.
HERB AND JACK: Great!
PETER: Okay. See you guys later.
HERB AND JACK: See you.

exercise 2

Now you will hear five questions about the conversation. Listen to the questions. Then write answers to the questions on the lines below. Discuss your answers with your classmates.

1. Are all the students from Texas?
2. Will the three students have lunch together?
3. Do all the students live on the same floor?
4. What do two of the students want to do?
5. Why does Peter think that Herb is from Texas?

Stress, page 3

In spoken English, important words are *stressed*. This means they are spoken louder, longer, or higher than other (unstressed) words. Stressed words usually give the most important information.

examples: My náme is Tóm.

We're on the sáme flóor.

Now listen to the first part of the conversation again. Some of the stressed words are missing. Repeat each sentence during the pause. Then fill in the missing stressed words.

JACK: Hi! How're you doing?
PETER: Oh, hi! You're Jack, right?
JACK: That's right. What's your name again?
PETER: Peter. Peter Riley.
JACK: Peter, this is my roommate, Herb.
PETER: Hi, Herb.
HERB: Nice to meet you.
PETER: Are you from Texas?
HERB: Yeah. Why? Do you think I have an accent?
PETER: Yeah.
HERB: Ha! You're the ones with the accent!

exercise 4

Now listen to the rest of the conversation. Mark the stressed words as in the example.

JACK: Lísten, Peter. We're really húngry. Do you want to get something to eát with us?
PETER: I can't. I have to meet my new roommate.
HERB: Oh, yeah? Well, okay. Listen, stop by and see us. We're up in 212.
PETER: Hey, we're on the same floor. Room 220.
HERB AND JACK: Great!
PETER: Okay. See you guys later.
HERB AND JACK: See you.

Reductions, page 4

In spoken English, important words are usually stressed. Many words that are not stressed are often *reduced*.

examples: Do you ... → D'ya ...

How are you doing? → How're ya doing?

exercise 5

Listen to these examples of reductions from the conversation. Repeat them after the speaker.

JACK: Hi! How're ya doing?
JACK: Peter, this's my roommate, Herb.
HERB: Nice ta meetcha.
PETER: Are ya from Texas?
JACK: D'ya wanna get something to eat with us?
PETER: I hafta meet my new roommate.

exercise 6

Listen to the reductions in these sentences. Write the long forms in the blanks. You may want to repeat the sentences for pronunciation practice.

1. How're ya feeling?
2. See ya in an hour.
3. Jack, d'ya wanna eat at the cafeteria?
4. When d'ya have ta meet your roommate?

Pronunciation of the -s ending, page 6

The -s ending is pronounced three ways, according to the end of the word:

/iz/ after -ch, -sh, -s, -x, and -z endings.

examples: teaches, uses, boxes

/s/ after voiceless -p, -t, -k, or -f endings.

examples: drinks, speaks, hits

/z/ after voiced consonant endings.

examples: carries, brings, runs

exercise 7

Listen to the following words. Check the sound you hear. The first one is done as an example.

1. plays
2. misses
3. hopes
4. stops

5. drives
6. phones
7. washes
8. summarizes

PART two   *Summarizing Main Ideas, page 6*

exercise 1

You are going to listen to a short speech. You will not understand every word. Before you listen, think about these questions.

1. Who is speaking?
2. Who is listening to the speech?
3. Where are they?

Now listen to the speech.

> Welcome to Faber College, one of the world's great schools of higher learning. We hope your stay here will be profitable and enjoyable both in your academic and your social endeavors.
>
> To help you find your way around the campus, we have designed a comprehensive tour that will begin shortly. Your guides will be waiting for you outside in fifteen minutes.

exercise 2

What information did the speaker give in the speech? Circle *yes* or *no*.

1. Welcome to Faber College.
2. Faber is a great school.
3. We hope you like it.
4. A campus tour begins in fifteen minutes.

If you answered *yes* to all statements, you understood the *main* or *important* ideas. *Remember* you don't need to understand all the words to understand the main message.

Now listen to the full speech again. Focus on the main ideas only.

exercise 3 Later on the campus tour, one of the students asks the tour guide this question: "Can you give us an idea of some good places to eat?" Listen to the guide's answer. Write the key words. The answer has two parts.

> Part A: There're lots of restaurants all over campus. If you're looking for something hot to eat, you can try the science building, the student union, or the Jones Hall cafeteria. A good place for salads is the new snack bar near the gym.
>
> Part B: If you're interested in a really good cup of coffee, then I recommend the North Campus Espresso Bar. They also have great ice cream, but only in the summer months. Don't try the hamburgers; they're really terrible.

PART three *Guessing Information, page 7*

Focus on Testing

Jack, Peter, and Kenji are talking. Listen to their conversation. The conversation has five parts, with a question at the end of each part. When you hear a question, circle the correct answer a, b, or c below. Then listen to the next part of the conversation, which contains the correct answer to the previous question. The first one is done as an example.

PETER: Let's get one with extra cheese on it.
JACK: And mushrooms and tomatoes too. I'm so hungry, I could eat a horse!

1. Where are Jack and Peter?

PETER: The pizza in this place is really terrific!
PETER: So, what do you think of that T.A. in chem class?
PETER: Well, he isn't as interesting as Professor Murphy, but he spends a lot of time correcting our homework and he really seems to know the subject.

2. What is a T.A.?

KENJI: There aren't any teaching assistants in my old university in Japan. The professors teach all the classes.
JACK: Are classes very different there?
KENJI: Well, yes! For example, students don't ask many questions in lectures and never interrupt the professor.
PETER: Oh, that's very common here.

3. How does Kenji feel about students interrupting lectures?

KENJI: I know it's common, but it's still a little unusual for me. In some ways, I think it's a good idea. Oh, before I forget, do you know how to reserve a tennis court?
PETER: You have to get a card at the recreation center. And, after that, you can call your reservation in.

4. How can students with recreation cards make reservations?

PETER: Here's the phone number for reservations.

JACK: Herb and I have a court for tomorrow afternoon. Do you guys want to play doubles with us?

PETER: Sounds good to me.

KENJI: Losers buy lunch.

5. What will probably happen tomorrow?

JACK AND HERB: You're on!

PETER: See you guys at the court . . .

JACK: . . . at 2:30.

PART **four** *Listening Tasks, page 8*

activity 1

Peter and Kenji have an answering machine. When they are not home, the machine records telephone messages for them. Listen to the people who call. Are they friends? Classmates? Parents? What are they calling about? Who gets more messages, Peter or Kenji? Complete the form for each message with the important information. The first one is done as an example.

WOMAN: Kenji, this is Linda from Dr. Brown's office. I'm calling to change your appointment. Unfortunately, Dr. Brown can't see you at two o'clock on Tuesday, but I can give you an appointment for Wednesday at two. I hope that's convenient for you. Please let us know at 855-7962.

WOMAN: 1. Peter, this is Nancy from your math class. Remember me? I'm, calling about this week's homework. I'm still sick and will probably stay home until Monday. So can you call me at 657-4940 any time before eleven? Thanks.

MAN: 2. Hi, Peter, it's Bud. Listen, wanna go to see Michael Jackson Saturday? He's singing at the Roxy Auditorium, and my cousin has an extra ticket. Give me a call if you want it. I'm at Sheri's house, and her number is 381-2644. The concert starts at eight-thirty, by the way. Talk to you later.

WOMAN: 3. I'm Mrs. Henry from the foreign student office, returning Kenji Suzuki's call. I'm sorry, but we still don't have your transcripts. Sometimes the mail is very slow, so wait a couple of weeks before you fill out another request form. And call me at extension 4745 if you have any questions.

MAN: 4. This is the research library calling. Peter Riley, we have a biology book with your name and number in it. You can pick it up at the front desk; just show your student identification. Ask for Edna or Dick.

MAN: 5. Hello, Peter. My name is Kevin Potter. My adviser gave me your number. I need help in math before my midterm exam. Can you let me know if you're available and how much you charge for tutoring? My number is 278-1861. Thanks. Bye.

MAN: 6. Kenji, this is Avi's Garage calling. We checked your car and it works fine. You can pick it up . . . eh . . . let's see. It's one-thirty now. How about around five o'clock? Oh, and there's a $25 service charge.

activity 2   Herb calls the college about a parking permit and talks to a secretary. Listen to the conversation and complete the application below.

SECRETARY: What's your name, please?

HERB: Herbert G. Myers: M-Y-E-R-S.

SECRETARY: What's your middle initial again?

HERB: G as in George.

SECRETARY: Address?

HERB: Hershey Hall. Room 212.

SECRETARY: Do you have a phone there?

HERB: Yeah, uh 825-3001, uh, extension 212.

SECRETARY: Okay. What's the year and make of your car?

HERB: '92 Toyota Celica.

SECRETARY: License plate?

HERB: AWJ 130

SECRETARY: One-thirty or one-thirteen?

HERB: One, three, oh.

SECRETARY: Okay. That'll be $80 for the semester or $160 for the year.

HERB: I just need it for the fall.

SECRETARY: All right. When we receive your check or money order for $80, we'll send you a permit for lot number nine.

HERB: Thank you very much.

SECRETARY: You're welcome.

HERB: Bye.

CHAPTER two

Experiencing Nature

Getting the Main Idea

exercise 1

Peter, Herb, and a friend, Mike, are going camping for the weekend. They are having a conversation in the car. Close your book and listen to their conversation. You may not understand every word. Listen for the main ideas.

PETER: I hate to drive in traffic like this.
MIKE: Especially when it's raining.
HERB: You think this is bad? Back in Texas a little rain like this is nothing!
PETER: Really? Isn't Texas hot and dry?
HERB: Oh, we have all kinds of weather in Texas. In the summer it's so hot you can fry an egg on the street. And in the winter it snows in some places.
MIKE: Well, you never see pictures of skiing cowboys.
HERB: Ha-ha! Real funny.
MIKE: Boy, this road is narrow. Be careful! We don't want to spend the week in the hospital.
HERB: So when do you think we'll get to Bald Mountain?
PETER: Not before midnight.
HERB: Then let's stay in a motel tonight.
PETER: Yeah, it doesn't look like the weather is going to clear up.
MIKE: And I'm not sleeping out in the woods until I hear the weather report.

exercise 2

Now you will hear six questions about the conversation. Listen to the questions. Then write answers to the questions on the lines below. Discuss your answers with your classmates.

   1. What's the weather like?
   2. Does this look like a lot of rain to Herb?
   3. What is the weather like in Texas?
   4. Where are they going?
   5. Why are they going to stay in a motel?
   6. Before sleeping out in the woods, what does Mike want to hear?

Stress, page 15

exercise 3

Now listen to the first part of the conversation again. Repeat each sentence during the pause. Then fill in the missing stressed words.

PETER: I hate to drive in traffic like this.
MIKE: Especially when it's raining.
HERB: You think this is bad? Back in Texas a little rain like this is nothing!

PETER: Really? Isn't Texas hot and dry?

HERB: Oh, we have all kinds of weather in Texas. In the summer it's so hot you can fry an egg on the street. And in the winter it snows in some places.

MIKE: Well, you never see pictures of skiing cowboys.

HERB: Ha-ha! Real funny.

exercise 4   Now listen to the rest of the conversation. Mark the stressed words.

MIKE: Boy, this road is narrow. Be careful! We don't want to spend the week in the hospital.

HERB: So when do you think we'll get to Bald Mountain?

PETER: Not before midnight.

HERB: Then let's stay in a motel tonight.

PETER: Yeah, it doesn't look like the weather is going to clear up.

MIKE: And I'm not sleeping out in the woods until I hear the weather report.

Can vs. Can't, page 16

exercise 5   Now listen to and repeat each statement. Circle *yes* if the statement is affirmative and *no* if the statement is negative. The first one is done as an example.

1. She can't swim very well.
2. Mike can drive.
3. The boys can cook.
4. I can't find his phone number.
5. Kenji can't speak Spanish.

6. He can speak Japanese.
7. I can't understand him.
8. Pete can come with us.
9. She can't take photographs in the rain.
10. Herb can play tennis very well.

Reductions, page 17

exercise 6   Listen to these examples of reductions from the conversation. Repeat them after the speaker.

We 'ave all kindza weather in Texas.

When d'ya think we'll get to Bald Mountain?

We don't wanna spend the week in the hospital.

It doesn't look like the weather is gonna clear up.

exercise 7   Listen to the reductions in the following conversation. Write the long forms in the blanks. You may want to repeat the sentences for pronunciation practice.

PETER: What d'ya 'ave in the car?

GAIL: We 'ave all kindza stuff.

PETER: D'ya have any drinks?

GAIL: Sure. What d'ya wanna have?

PETER: How 'bouta Coke?

exercise 1   Peter, Mike, and Herb are at a motel. They see a man and a woman talking to the manager. The man and the woman look tired but excited. Listen to their story.

WOMAN: You're not going to believe this! It's the most incredible thing! We're camping nearby. About an hour ago we get back to our camp after hiking all afternoon in that awful rain and . . .

MAN: Yeah, all wet and everything.

WOMAN: Right. So we want to get into some dry clothes, of course. And we go into our tent to change, but we can't find our clothes! So we go back outside to look around. Then we see the craziest thing. From out of the woods two great big brown bears come walking toward us wearing—you're not going to believe it—wearing our clothes!

MANAGER: Ah, come on, that's ridiculous. What do you mean—bears wearing your clothes?

MAN: Well, one bear has my T-shirt wrapped around his neck; the other has Mary's pants over his head. We still don't know where the rest of our clothes are!

MANAGER: (sound of laughing)

WOMAN: It's funny to *you*, but boy were we scared!

exercise 2   Now you will hear just the key sentences of the same story. As you listen, look at the key verbs below. Take notes to help you retell the story. Don't try to copy complete sentences. For example, after the verb hike, you might write *man and woman hike in rain.*

WOMAN: • We get back to our camp after hiking all afternoon in that awful rain.
- We want to get into some dry clothes, so we go into our tent to change.
- We can't find our clothes, so we go back outside to look around.
- Then we see the craziest thing—two great big brown bears walking toward us.
- You're not going to believe it—wearing our clothes!
- It's funny to you, but boy, were we scared!

PART **three** *Guessing Information, page 18*

Focus on Testing

Peter, Mike, and Herb are camping in the woods. Listen to their conversation. When you hear a question, circle the correct answer. Then listen to the next part of the conversation, which will contain the correct answer to the previous question.

HERB: That looks really good.

PETER: Hmm . . . and it smells terrific too. How do you make it, Mike?

MIKE: I can't tell you. It's a family secret. Wait until you taste it. It's delicious!

1. What is Mike doing?

HERB: So how long are you going to cook this fish?

MIKE: Don't worry. It'll be ready in a couple of minutes.

PETER: I feel really worn out.

HERB: Me too! It's nice to just sit here and rest!

2. Peter and Herb are all worn out. What does that mean?

MIKE: You guys are tired? And how do you think I feel? I'm doing all the cooking!
PETER: Yeah, we know. So let's just eat and go to bed.
HERB: Bed? That's what I need, a real bed. My back still hurts from last night.
MIKE: Yeah, all those rocks under the tent!
PETER: And bugs everywhere!

3. The boys are sleeping outside. How do they feel about it?

MIKE: Well, camping is uncomfortable sometimes, but I still enjoy it. So what's our plan for tomorrow?
PETER: Let's get up early and get to Bald Peak by lunchtime.
HERB: Isn't it cold and windy up there?
MIKE: Yeah, but I promise you, the view is fantastic. On a clear day, you can see the whole valley below.

4. Where do they plan to go tomorrow?

MIKE: The top of Bald Mountain is really beautiful. It'll be a great place to take some shots.
PETER: Do you still have some film left?
MIKE: I think so.
PETER: Don't worry. If you don't have any, you can buy some postcards of the mountain back at the park tourist center.

5. What does Mike want to do?

MIKE: Postcards? They're not the same as your own photographs.

PART **four** *Listening Tasks, page 19*

activity 1

Mike is listening to the weather forecast on the radio. Listen to the information and use the chart to take notes about the weekend weather.

This is the National Weather Service report at five in the afternoon, Friday. The forecast for the Bald Mountain area is partly cloudy with some showers through the night, clearing by early morning. The high today was sixty-one degrees; overnight lows will be in the mid-fifties. Tomorrow's highs will be in the sixties with fair skies continuing throughout the day. Temperatures will drop Saturday night to a chilly low of forty-five degrees. Sunday will continue fair, warming up to a high temperature of seventy degrees. Sunday night lows will get down below fifty again. There will be a fifty percent chance of rain on Monday.

activity 2

Listen to the following conversations about the weather. Write the key words that help you know what season it is. Then write the name of the season. The first one is done as an example.

CONVERSATION 1

A: Nice weather we're having.
B: Yes. Isn't it a nice surprise? At this time it's usually much cooler and raining already.
A: Well, this weather will probably end soon; all the leaves on the trees are brown.

CONVERSATION 2

A: Take your coat; it's freezing outside.
B: Nah, I'm only going to the corner store.
A: I'm telling you, it's in the low thirties out there.

CONVERSATION 3

A: How do you like all this rain?
B: Well, it's good for the trees and flowers.
A: Yes, it's nice to see the leaves coming back on the trees again.

CONVERSATION 4

A: Is it hot enough for you?
B: Whew . . . it sure is. I don't mind the heat so much. It's the humidity that bothers me. Look, I'm all wet.
A: Me too. Let's go get a cold drink somewhere.

activity **3**   Listen to more conversations about the weather. Circle the temperature you hear.

CONVERSATION 1

A: What's the weather like today?
B: Hot and humid and about ninety-five degrees.

CONVERSATION 2

A: I'm gonna take a swim. Wanna come?
B: Is the pool heated?
A: Sure. It's probably over eighty degrees.

CONVERSATION 3

A: How was your ski holiday?
B: Great! The weather was in the thirties and we had perfect snow conditions.

CONVERSATION 4

A: Let's go for a walk.
B: What's it like out?
A: About forty degrees but the wind stopped.
B: Thanks. I think I'll pass.

CONVERSATION 5

A: It's a hundred and three in here! Why don't you turn on the air conditioning?
B: It's broken.

CONVERSATION 6

A: How was the weather in Europe this summer?
B: Just lovely. Sunny but never over thirty degrees.
A: Thirty?? Oh, you mean Celsius.

CONVERSATION 7

A: What's wrong?
B: It's thirteen below outside and I can't find my gloves.
A: Here. Use mine. I have an extra pair.

CONVERSATION 8

A: Did you check the weather forecast?
B: Yeah. It's supposed to be in the high seventies this weekend.
A: The seventies?? I guess we can forget about skiing.

CHAPTER three

Living to Eat or Eating to Live?

Getting the Main Idea

exercise 1

Mr. and Mrs. Nutley are doing their weekly grocery shopping. Close your book and listen to their conversation. You may not understand every word. Listen for the main ideas.

MR. N: Well, dear, I got a few things that aren't on the grocery list.

MRS. N: I can see that! You're not shopping for an army, you know.

MR. N: You know I always do this when I'm hungry.

MRS. N: Well, let's see what you have here.

MR. N: Some nice, fresh strawberries for only 99 cents.

MRS. N: Well, that's okay. But why do you have all these cookies?

MR. N: I don't know; don't you like them?

MRS. N: Oh, I suppose. I hope you have a box of soap here.

MR. N: Sure—a large one.

MRS. N: That steak looks really expensive!

MR. N: Well, it isn't. It's just $3 a pound.

MRS. N: What's this? More ice cream? We already have a gallon at home. Put it back and hand me my checkbook.

CASHIER: I'm sorry, ma'am; this is the express line. You have too many groceries, and we don't take checks here.

exercise 2

Now you will hear six questions about the conversation. Listen to the questions. Then write answers to the questions on the lines below. Discuss your answers with your classmates.

1. Why is Mr. Nutley buying so much food?
2. How much are the strawberries?
3. Does Mr. Nutley have a small box of soap?
4. What does Mrs. Nutley say about the steak?
5. Is the steak expensive?
6. Are Mr. and Mrs. Nutley in the correct line?

Stress, page 27

exercise 3

Listen to the first part of the conversation again. Repeat each sentence during the pause. Remember to pronounce stressed words *louder, longer,* and *higher.* Then fill in the missing stressed words.

MR. N: Well, dear, I got a few things that aren't on the grocery list.

MRS. N: I can see that! You're not shopping for an army, you know.

MR. N: You know I always do this when I'm hungry.

MRS. N: Well, let's see what you have here.

MR. N: Some nice, fresh strawberries for only 99 cents.

MRS. N: Well, that's okay. But why do you have all these cookies?

MR. N: I don't know; don't you like them?

exercise **4**   Now listen to the rest of the conversation. Mark the stressed words.

MRS. N: Oh, I suppose. I hope you have a box of soap here.

MR. N: Sure—a large one.

MRS. N: That steak looks really expensive!

MR. N: Well, it isn't. It's just $3 a pound.

MRS. N: What's this? More ice cream? We already have a gallon at home. Put it back and hand me my checkbook.

CASHIER: I'm sorry, ma'am; this is the express line. You have too many groceries, and we don't take checks here.

Teens or Tens, page 28

exercise **5**   Listen to these sentences. Write the number you hear on the blank line in each picture. The first one is done as an example.

1. This turkey weighs 14 pounds.
2. The market is open until 10:30.
3. We spent $40 on groceries yesterday.
4. This milk is good until November 13th.
5. Those peaches cost $1.90 a pound.
6. Everything in this store is about 15 percent cheaper today.
7. My daughter is getting married. I need 30 bottles of champagne.
8. Please hurry up. The store will close in 15 minutes.
9. By using this coupon, you can save 70 cents on this ice cream.
10. Canned vegetables are on aisle 19.

Reductions, page 29

exercise **6**   Listen to these examples of reductions from the conversation. Repeat them after the speaker.

Let's see watcha have here.
Why d'ya have all these cookies?
I dunno.
Doncha like 'em?

exercise **7**   Listen to the reductions in the following conversation. Write the long forms in the blanks. You may want to repeat the sentences for pronunciation practice.

CUSTOMER: Waiter!

WAITER: Yes sir. Do you know whatcha want?

CUSTOMER: D'ya have any fresh whitefish?

WAITER: Yes, we catch 'em fresh every day.

CUSTOMER: Great, I'll have some.

WAITER: What kind of wine d'ya want with that?

CUSTOMER: I dunno. Why doncha recommend something?

WAITER: Our California wines are excellent.

exercise 1   Many Americans worry about how much they weigh. In fact, about a third of the American people are overweight, and this number is increasing. Listen to the following advice about losing weight. Take notes on the do's and don'ts.

Do you think you're overweight? Are you thinking of going on a diet? Here are some things you should and shouldn't do when trying to lose weight. First, the best way to lose weight safely is to lose it slowly. This means about 2 pounds a week, no more. If you lose weight too quickly, you'll probably gain it back anyway. So how do you lose weight slowly? First, eat right. Stay away from fast foods and prepackaged foods—you know, canned and frozen stuff. They may save you time, but they're bad for your health because they're high in fat and salt. In addition to changing your eating habits, you should also exercise regularly. To lose 1 pound, you must burn about 3,500 calories. You can burn about half of that just by exercising for 30 minutes, three times a week. Stay away from diet pills and crash diets. Diet pills can be very dangerous. They can affect your muscles, bones, and organs like your heart. They can even cause death. Crash diets promise quick results in a very short time, but don't try them; the results don't last. Remember, the best way to lose weight is to eat right, exercise, and be patient.

exercise 2   Kenji and his friends are shopping at the Shop-and-Save Department Store. They hear some announcements. Before you listen, talk with a partner about what kinds of things stores announce to their shoppers—for example, special sales, store hours, etc. Then listen to the tape.

Good afternoon, shoppers. We hope you like our improved and expanded store. For your convenience, our new hours are from ten in the morning to midnight, seven days a week. At this time, we have a special sale in our shoe department. All boots there are going for half price. That's right! Fifty percent off! That's like buying the left boot and getting the right one free!

Also, don't forget to stop by our sportswear department for this summer's styles in tennis and beach wear. Remember, all our friendly cashiers are ready to stamp your parking ticket for two hours of free parking.

Our food section next door has a new bakery. We also feature fresh produce and a fish market.

And . . . oh . . . there is a little blond boy named Brian looking for his mother. Will you please pick him up in the toy department on the main floor?

exercise 3   Listen to the announcements again. Write down the important information. Don't copy sentences; just write your notes below.

Focus on Testing

In this section, you will hear four conversations. As you listen to each one, decide where the people are eating and circle the correct answer. Then listen to the next conversation, which contains the correct answer to the previous question.

WAITER: Good evening. My name is Pierre. Would you like a cocktail?

BOB: No, thanks. But we would like to see the wine list.

WAITER: Certainly. And here are your menus. Our specialties tonight are lemon chicken and fresh broiled swordfish.

1. The speakers are in a . . .

SUSAN: Thanks for dinner, Bob. This was a wonderful restaurant.

FELIPE: Why don't we sit at the counter? There aren't any free tables.
SALIM: Fine.
WAITRESS: Coffee?
FELIPE: Yes.
SALIM: Yes, please.
WAITRESS: I'll be right back to get your order.

2. The speakers are in a . . .

FELIPE: This coffee shop is always crowded because the prices are so low.

A: These salads look great. Do you want one?
B: No, I want a hot dish from over here.
SERVER: Yes, what would you like?
A: Is that mushroom soup?
SERVER: No, it's bean soup.
A: How much is it?
SERVER: It's a dollar a bowl. You pay down there at the cashier.

3. The speakers are in a . . .

B: I hear this cafeteria is open all night.

WAITER: May I take your order?
JOHN: I'll have two superburgers, no onions, and two small Cokes.
WAITER: Here or to go?
JOHN: Here. And an order of fries.
WAITER: That'll be $4.

4. The speakers are in a . . .

JOHN: I know fast foods are bad for you, but I love this place.

PART **four**   *Listening Tasks, page 32*

activity 1

Tom is teaching Kenji how to cook. Listen to the recipe for French toast and take notes.

TOM: To make French toast for four, you'll need two eggs, one cup milk, one-half teaspoon of salt, and about a tablespoon of butter. First, beat the eggs, milk, and salt with a fork for a minute until they're well mixed. Then melt the butter in a frying pan. When the butter is hot, dip eight slices of bread into the egg mixture and fry them until golden brown. Serve them on a warm plate with butter and syrup or jam.

***activity* 2**

Mr. and Mrs. Nutley plan to drive around the United States soon. Their niece, Paula, is a chef. She tells them about foods popular in different parts of the country. Take a look at the map below of the United States and Canada. As you hear the name of each food, write it on the map in the place where it is popular.

PAULA: Vancouver, in Western Canada, has delicious Chinese food. San Francisco also has excellent Chinese and Japanese restaurants. Northern California has better wine than almost anywhere; they make wine in Napa and Sonoma. If you get to Texas, be sure to eat some Mexican food. It's very spicy, but delicious. In the Midwest, you can find terrific cheese in Wisconsin. And don't forget to have steak in Chicago. The beef is very good there. If you drive to the Northeast, try some Maine lobster. It's superb. And in Montreal, Canada, the French food is fabulous. Oh, and if you decide to go down south to Georgia, fried chicken is very popular. And in Florida, of course, you'll find the best oranges.

MR. NUTLEY: That's enough for now, Paula. I'm feeling full already.

CHAPTER four

Getting Around the Community

Getting the Main Idea

exercise 1

Herb and Mike live in a small college town near a big city. Mike is going into the city today. Close your book and listen to their conversation. You may not understand every word. Listen for the main ideas.

HERB: Say, Mike. Can you give me some help with my math homework this afternoon?

MIKE: Uum, I'd like to, but I really can't. I have to go into the city and do a lot of things.

HERB: Oh yeah? Like what?

MIKE: I have to go to the bank and open a checking account, I have to mail a package at the post office, and I might get a haircut too.

HERB: Well, that's not much. When are you going to come back?

MIKE: I'm not sure. I might eat downtown if the traffic looks bad.

HERB: How are you going to get around?

MIKE: I don't know. I think I'll take a taxi.

HERB: Why don't you take the bus; it's much cheaper.

MIKE: Maybe I will. Can I get you anything?

HERB: Let me see . . . Could you get me some stamps?

MIKE: Sure.

HERB: And would you buy me some tennis balls?

MIKE: Okay.

HERB: Oh, yeah . . . and our camping pictures are ready. Would you pick them up if you can?

MIKE: Is that all, boss?

HERB: Yes, for now.

exercise 2

Now you will hear five questions about the conversation. Listen to the questions. Then write answers to the questions on the lines below. Discuss your answers with your classmates.

1. Is Mike going to help Herb this afternoon?
2. Why is Mike going into the city?
3. Where is Mike going to have dinner?
4. How is Mike going to get downtown?
5. What will Mike do for Herb?

Stress, page 39

exercise 3

Listen to the first part of the conversation again. Repeat each sentence during the pause. Then fill in the missing stressed words.

HERB: Say, Mike. Can you give me some help with my math homework this afternoon?
MIKE: Uum, I'd like to, but I really can't. I have to go into the city and do a lot of things.
HERB: Oh yeah? Like what?
MIKE: I have to go to the bank and open a checking account, I have to mail a package at the post office, and I might get a haircut too.
HERB: Well, that's not much. When are you going to come back?
MIKE: I'm not sure. I might eat downtown if the traffic looks bad.
HERB: How are you going to get around?
MIKE: I don't know. I think I'll take a taxi.

exercise 4   Now listen to the rest of the conversation. Mark the stressed words.

HERB: Why don't you take the bus; it's much cheaper.
MIKE: Maybe I will. Can I get you anything?
HERB: Let me see . . . Could you get me some stamps?
MIKE: Sure.
HERB: And would you buy me some tennis balls?
MIKE: Okay.
HERB: Oh, yeah . . . and our camping pictures are ready. Would you pick them up if you can?
MIKE: Is that all, boss?
HERB: Yes, for now.

Reductions, page 40

exercise 5   Listen to these examples of reductions from the conversation. Repeat them after the speaker.

Kinya gimme some help?
I'd liketa, but I can't.
I hafta go into the city and do a lotta things.
When are ya gonna come back?
Howaya gonna get around?
Can I getcha anything?
Couldja get me some stamps?
And wouldja buy me some tennis balls?
Pick 'em up if you can.

exercise 6   Listen to the reductions in the following conversation. Write the long forms in the blanks. You may want to repeat the sentences for pronunciation practice.

ANA: Canya show me where the bus stops?
SUE: I'd liketa, but I really don't know. You'll hafta ask someone else. Or I can getcha some bus maps.
ANA: Forget it; you're gonna be late.
SUE: No, I don't hafta rush.
ANA: Okay. Wouldja please get 'em, then?
SUE: Sure, I'll pick 'em right up.
ANA: Wouldja bring an extra for my friend?

PART two   *Summarizing Main Ideas, page 41*

exercise 1   Mike is back after a long afternoon in the city. He looks tired and unhappy. Listen to his conversation with his friends.

MIKE: Phew . . . I'm glad I don't live in the city. The traffic there is terrible. And I have a headache from the noise and all the smog.

HERB: You think this is bad? Ask Kenji about Tokyo.

KENJI: Yeah, Tokyo is noisier and much more crowded than the city here.

HERB: Yeah, and I hear the smog's worse too.

KENJI: That's right.

MIKE: So, I guess you don't miss that, huh?

KENJI: Well, I don't miss those things, but a city like Tokyo is also very exciting.

MIKE: Yes, I'm sure that's true. But I prefer the peace and quiet of a town like ours.

KENJI: Well, I like it here too. The people are friendlier and things are cheaper.

HERB: Well, you know, I'm from a small town, and it can be awfully conservative and boring. I'm ready to live in a big city like New York or Chicago. And you can make more money there.

MIKE: Yeah, but it's more dangerous there.

HERB: Yeah, that's a disadvantage. But there are lots of good things too.

MIKE: Yeah? Like what? The long lines you wait in at the bank or in the stores?

HERB: Lines don't bother me. I really love shopping in the city. You can find anything.

MIKE: Great! Then next time we need something, you can go into the city.

exercise 2   Now listen again. List the good things and the bad things you hear about cities and towns. A few examples are already written in.

PART three   *Guessing Information, page 42*

Focus on Testing

Listen to the following conversations, which take place in different parts of the city. When you hear a question, circle the correct answer. Then listen to the next line of the conversation, which contains the correct answer to the previous question.

A: Next, please

B: I'd like to cash this.

A: Sure. Don't forget to sign the back. Do you have an account here?

B: Not at this branch.

A: Then I'll have to see your driver's license.

    1. Where are the speakers?

B: How late is this bank open?

A: Excuse me. Do you stop at Third and Highland?

B: Yes, ma'am . . . Passengers, please move to the rear.

A: Could you tell me when to get off?

B: Sure.

    2. Where is the woman?

A: Is the bus always this crowded?

A: Can I help you?

B: Yes, I've got four shirts here and two pairs of pants and a jacket. I'm leaving town in a few days, so can I pick them up tomorrow?

A: We can have the pants ready, but the shirts won't be back until Wednesday mornng.

B: Well, okay. Oh, and don't forget to take out this coffee stain.

3. Where are the speakers?

A: No problem. We're the best dry cleaners in town.

A: Fill out this application and wait in line B for your eye test.

B: About how long will this take?

A: Well, you'll have to take a fifteen-minute road test, and the written test also takes fifteen minutes. But you may have to wait in line a long time for your picture.

4. What is the young man doing?

B: When will you send me my driver's license?

A: Will this get to New York in three days?

B: Only if you send it special delivery.

A: Okay. I'd like to do that.

B: All right. Anything else?

A: Yes. Give me a book of first class stamps and three aerograms, please.

B: Fine, that's uh, twelve dollars and two cents, please.

5. Where are the speakers?

A: Is this post office open on Saturdays?

PART **four** *Listening Tasks, page 43*

activity 1

Mike is getting directions to various places in the city. Right now, he is at Joe's Diner on Columbus Street. Look at the map and follow the directions you hear. On the map, in the correct location, write the name of each place Mike goes to.

MIKE: Excuse me. Is there a bank near here?

MAN: Sure. There's one four or five blocks from here. Walk north on Newbury Boulevard to First Street; turn right on First. At the second block, turn left and look for the bank on the right side of Walnut Street just before Cherry Lane.

You are at location C. Continue to the next place from here.

MIKE: Excuse me, ma'am. Is there a big department store nearby?

WOMAN: There's one on the corner of Newbury and Cherry. Just walk down Cherry two blocks and turn left. Then you'll see it on the left.

You are at location A. Continue to the next place from here.

MIKE: What's the best way to get to King's Books? I hear it's a great bookstore.
MAN: Oh, yes. They've got everything. You know how to get to Washington Boulevard?
MIKE: I think so. I go out on First Street and turn right.
MAN: Nope. Turn left. Washington's the first street. Turn right on Washington and follow it a couple of blocks to Columbus Street. Turn left and cross Walnut Street. On the left side you'll see a barbershop and then a market. Walk between then, and you'll find the bookstore in back.

You are at location F. Continue to the next place from here.

MIKE: Can you recommend a Chinese restaurant near here?
WOMAN: Sure. Chow's has good Chinese food.
MIKE: How do I get there?
WOMAN: Go out to Walnut Street and go up to Second Street. Walk west, cross Washington Boulevard, and the restaurant is across from Mort's Gym.
MIKE: So it's on the south side of the street?
WOMAN: That's right.

You are at location E. Continue to the next place from here.

MIKE: Is there a concert in the park tonight?
MAN: I think so.
MIKE: How do I get there?
MAN: Are you driving?
MIKE: No, I'm walking.
MAN: Turn right and walk all the way to McMillan Road. Then make a left and go straight a block or two. The park is on the corner of Cherry Lane and McMillan.

You have arrived at location H. Stop and relax.

activity **2**

If you need directions, your local bus company can help you. Just tell them where you want to leave from, where you want to go, and what time you need to get there. Listen to the following telephone conversations with the Metro Bus Company. Take notes on each conversation.

CONVERSATION 1

A: Metro Bus Company.
B: Hello. I need to go to the airport from Main Street.
A: Main Street and what?
B: Main and Grant.
A: Okay. What time do you have to be at the airport?
B: At six o'clock.
A: Take bus thirty-three at four-fifty at the corner of Main and Grant. Get off at Airport Boulevard. That's two blocks from the airport.
B: So it's bus number thirty-three at four-fifty; and I get off at . . .
A: Airport Boulevard.
B: Thank you very much.

CONVERSATION 2

A: Bus information. Tom speaking.
B: I want to go to Salem. Is there a bus at around nine in the morning?

A: Just a minute. . . . There's one at eight-fifty, leaving from the Hilton Hotel.

B: I see. What's the fare?

A: It's $7 one way.

B: How long does it take?

A: About forty minutes.

B: Thanks.

CONVERSATION 3

A: Metro Bus Company. May I help you?

B: How can I get to 1800 Orange Street?

A: From where?

B: From Hollywood Boulevard. Hollywood and Temple.

A: Get on bus number one-oh-two at the corner of Hollywood and Temple. Get off at Madison Avenue and Orange, then walk two blocks north on Orange.

B: How often does the bus run?

A: Ah, let's see. Bus one-oh-two runs every six minutes.

B: Thanks.

CHAPTER five

Home

Getting the Main Idea

exercise 1

Peter and his friends are waiting for Mike at the cafeteria. Look at the picture and guess why Mike is late. Close your book and listen to their conversation. You may not understand every word. Listen for the main ideas.

JUDY: So where were you? We waited for an hour, but then we decided to have lunch without you.

MIKE: Sorry, guys. I had to help my sister move out of her old apartment.

PETER: Did you say your sister just moved?

MIKE: Yeah.

PETER: Where was her apartment?

MIKE: Right around the corner. Just five minutes away. Why?

PETER: My friend Barbara needs a place right away. How big is it?

MIKE: It's a one bedroom apartment with a small kitchen and bathroom. The living room has a fireplace.

PETER: Great! What did she pay there?

MIKE: Only six-fifty, but it might go up.

PETER: Could you give me the address for Barbara?

MIKE: Sure. It's 1213 Rose Avenue. Tell her to see the manager soon, before it's rented.

PETER: Okay. I'll call her right away.

exercise 2

Now you will hear seven questions about the conversation. Listen to the questions. Then write answers to the questions on the lines below. Discuss your answers with your classmates.

1. Is Mike looking for an apartment?
2. Where did Mike go?
3. Where was his sister's apartment?
4. Who is Barbara?
5. What does Barbara need?
6. How many bedrooms does the apartment have?
7. How much is the rent?

Stress, page 49

exercise 3

Listen to the first part of the conversation again. Repeat each sentence during the pause. Remember to pronounce stressed words *louder, longer,* and *higher.* Then fill in the missing stressed words.

JUDY: So where were you? We waited for an hour, but then we decided to have lunch without you.

MIKE: Sorry, guys. I had to help my sister move out of her old apartment.

PETER: Did you say your sister just moved?

MIKE: Yeah.

PETER: Where was her apartment?

MIKE: Right around the corner. Just five minutes away. Why?

exercise **4**   Now listen to the rest of the conversation. Mark the stressed words.

PETER: My friend Barbara needs a place right away. How big is it?

MIKE: It's a one bedroom apartment with a small kitchen and bathroom. The living room has a fireplace.

PETER: Great! What did she pay there?

MIKE: Only six-fifty, but it might go up.

PETER: Could you give me the address for Barbara?

MIKE: Sure. It's 1213 Rose Avenue. Tell her to see the manager soon, before it's rented.

PETER: Okay. I'll call her right away.

Reductions, page 50

exercise **5**   Listen to these examples of reductions from the conversation. Repeat them after the speaker.

Didja say your sister moved?
I hadta help.
She hadta get out.
I'was only six-fifty.
Couldja gimme the address?
Tell 'er to see the manager.
I'll call 'er right away.

exercise **6**   Listen to the reductions in the following conversation. Write the long forms in the blanks. You may want to repeat the sentences for pronunciation practice.

A: Didja get your new phone yet?

B: Yeah, but I hadta call the phone company three times. It was a real pain. Here's my new number. When you see Jane, couldja tell 'er my number too?

A: Sure. I'll see 'er at school tomorrow.

Pronunciation of the *-ed* Ending, page 51

The *-ed* ending is pronounced three ways, according to the end of the word:
/id/ after *-d* and *-t* endings.

examples: waited, invited, needed

/t/ after voiceless endings.

examples: fixed, watched, helped

/d/ after voiced consonant endings.

examples: lived, showed, listened

exercise 7   Listen to the following words. Check the sound you hear. The first one is done as an example.

1. turned
2. rented
3. mixed
4. asked
5. recommended

6. walked
7. tested
8. followed
9. moved

PART two   *Summarizing Main Ideas, page 51*

exercise 1   Barbara is looking at Marsha's old apartment. Listen as the manager shows Barbara around the apartment.

MANAGER: So, here is the living room. Oh, and please don't touch the walls; we've just painted them. I hope you like green. As you can see, there's lots of light in here. And there's the fireplace. It's great in the winter.

BARBARA: Whew, it's warm in here, isn't it? Is there any air conditioning?

MANAGER: No, just keep this window open. . . . Oh, it's almost never this noisy.

BARBARA: What did you say?

MANAGER: Come this way. . . . Here's your kitchen, all electric, a dishwasher. . . . You've got a big freezer, there's room for a table here . . .

BARBARA: That's nice. Could I see the bedroom?

MANAGER: It's over here. We just put in new carpeting, so we raised the rent $25.

BARBARA: Oh, really? Hmm . . . the bedroom looks a little small.

MANAGER: But look at the closet space! And here is your little bathroom.

BARBARA: Oh, what about that?

MANAGER: Hm . . . the plumber just fixed that last week. I'll have to call him again.

exercise 2   Listen again. Take notes about the good things and the bad things about the apartment. Two examples are already written in.

exercise 3   Mr. Nutley passes Barbara on his way into his apartment. Listen to their conversation once. Then listen to it again and take notes.

MR. NUTLEY: Oh, so you're my new neighbor.

BARBARA: Yes, I just moved in this week. I'm Barbara.

MR. NUTLEY: Nice to meet you, young lady. I'm Ed Nutley. My wife and I moved here seventeen years ago.

BARBARA: Wow. I bet you really know the neighborhood then, huh?

MR. NUTLEY: I sure do. It's very different now than it was in those days.

BARBARA: Oh? What do you mean?

MR. NUTLEY: Well, first of all, there used to be a beautiful park right across the street. It's that big parking lot now. And there wasn't a lot of traffic or noise back then. Also we used to have a lot of kids on this street. I sure miss them. We knew everybody in this building, but they all moved away. And these days nobody says hello anymore.

BARBARA: That's really too bad. I like to know my neighbors.

MR. NUTLEY: Good. Then come by this evening for cake and coffee and you can meet my wife.

BARBARA: Thanks. I will!

Focus on Testing

Mike's sister Marsha also found a new place to live. Listen to Mike and Marsha's conversation. Circle the correct answer to each question you hear. Then listen to the next part of the conversation, which gives you the correct answer to the previous question.

MARSHA: If you want to help unpack, you can put these out on the coffee table. I want to read them this week.

1. What is Marsha probably talking about?

MIKE: You always throw out half your magazines without ever looking at them. Now, do you want your TV in the living room?

MARSHA: No, not in here. Television helps me fall asleep at night.

2. Where does Marsha want the TV?

MIKE: I'll take it into the bedroom then. Wow, and I thought my bedroom was large! You could get lost in *here*.

3. What does Mike say about Marsha's bedroom?

MARSHA: Yes, it's really very big, isn't it? Well, I'm almost all moved in. You're right, you know . . . I'm really sad I left Rover with Mom. I'll miss his cold little nose waking me up in the morning. He used to sleep under my bed.

4. Who is Rover?

MIKE: Then why did you move here? The ad said, "Absolutely no dogs."

MARSHA: The rent was so great that I had to take it.

5. Why did Marsha take the apartment?

MIKE: Yeah, three-fifty a month for this is so low. I see what you mean.

activity 1

Barbara is going to move soon. She is calling the post office to tell them about her new address. A clerk is helping her fill out a change-of-address form. First listen to the conversation, but don't write. Listen for the main ideas. Then listen to the conversation again. This time, complete the form with the information you hear.

CLERK: What's your name, miss?

BARBARA: George.

CLERK: George?

BARBARA: Yeah. That's my last name.

CLERK: Oh. Can I have your first name and middle initial?

BARBARA: Barbara, A. A as in apple.

CLERK: What's your address?

BARBARA: Uh, . . . the old one or the new one?

CLERK: Give me the new one first.

BARBARA: 8535 Holloway.

CLERK: Is that two words?

BARBARA: No. One. H-O-L-L-O-W-A-Y. Holloway Drive.

CLERK: Holloway Drive. Right. And where is that?

BARBARA: That's Los Angeles, 90069.

CLERK: . . . six, nine. And what was your old address?

BARBARA: 802 University Avenue, uh . . . Los Angeles, 90308.

CLERK: 90038?

BARBARA: No, 90308.

CLERK: Oh. Okay. And when do you want your mail at your new address?

BARBARA: Can you start, uh, Monday?

CLERK: Sure. Let's see . . . uh, that's April 1. But you know you'll have to come in to sign this form before then . . .

BARBARA: Yeah, no problem. I'll be in before Monday to do that.

activity **2**

It's moving day. Look at Barbara's empty new apartment. First, listen to her instructions to the movers. Then listen again. This time, write the number of the item in the correct place on the picture.

MOVER: Where do you want the couch, miss?

BARBARA: How about here, where I'm standing.

MOVER: What about the TV?

BARBARA: Just put it beside the fireplace.

MOVER: And the bookshelf. I guess it goes in the living room too.

BARBARA: No, I want it in the bedroom.

MOVER: What about these towels?

BARBARA: Just put them in the bathroom.

MOVER: What's in these boxes? They're really heavy.

BARBARA: Careful! Those are my dishes. Just leave them on the kitchen counter. Where are the boxes with my books?

MOVER: They're next to the bed. And your clothes are there too. We put them on the bed. Is that okay?

BARBARA: Sure. Everything is a mess anyway.

Emergencies and Strange Experiences

PART **one** *Listening to Conversations, page 58*

Getting the Main Idea

exercise **1**   Peter and Herb are finishing a game of tennis. Close your book and listen to their conversation. You may not understand every word. Listen for the main ideas.

> PETER: Nice game!
>
> HERB: Oops . . . Ow—my leg!
>
> PETER: What's wrong? Where does it hurt, Herb?
>
> HERB: My knee. I think I broke it.
>
> WOMAN: Excuse me, can I help? I'm a doctor. I was playing over there when I heard you scream. What happened?
>
> HERB: I tried to jump over the net and I fell on my knee.
>
> WOMAN: Can you move it?
>
> HERB: I don't think so, and it *really* hurts.
>
> WOMAN: Let me have a look. Well, it may be broken.
>
> PETER: Do you want me to go call nine-one-one?
>
> WOMAN: No. There's a hospital right around the corner, so I don't think we'll need an ambulance. If you help me get your friend into my van, we can drive him over for some x-rays. The head of the emergency room is a friend of mine.
>
> PETER: That's terrific. We're really lucky you were here!
>
> HERB: We sure are. How can we thank you?
>
> WOMAN: Oh, I'm always happy to help out. But after you're better, if you want to give me a tennis lesson . . . Now let's get you up onto your good leg.

exercise **2**   Now you will hear six questions about the conversation. Listen to the questions. Then write answers to the questions on the lines below. Discuss your answers with your classmates.

1. What were Peter and Herb doing before the accident?
2. Who was hurt?
3. How did the accident happen?
4. Who came to help?
5. Why don't they need to call an ambulance?
6. What would the doctor like the boys to do for her?

Stress, page 59

exercise **3** Listen to the first part of the conversation again. Repeat each sentence during the pause. Remember to pronounce stressed words *louder, longer,* and *higher.* Then fill in the missing stressed words.

PETER: Nice game!

HERB: Oops . . . Ow—my leg!

PETER: What's wrong? Where does it hurt, Herb?

HERB: My knee. I think I broke it.

WOMAN: Excuse me, can I help? I'm a doctor. I was playing over there when I heard you scream. What happened?

HERB: I tried to jump over the net and I fell on my knee.

exercise **4** Now listen to the rest of the conversation. Mark the stressed words.

WOMAN: Can you move it?

HERB: I don't think so, and it really hurts.

WOMAN: Let me have a look. Well, it may be broken.

PETER: Do you want me to go call nine-one-one?

WOMAN: No. There's a hospital right around the corner, so I don't think we'll need an ambulance. If you help me get your friend into my van, we can drive him over for some x-rays. The head of the emergency room is a friend of mine.

PETER: That's terrific. We're really lucky you were here!

HERB: We sure are. How can we thank you?

WOMAN: Oh, I'm always happy to help out. But after you're better, if you want to give me a tennis lesson . . . Now let's get you up onto your good leg.

Reductions, page 60

exercise **5** Listen to these examples of reductions from the conversation. Repeat them after the speaker.

I heardja scream.
I triedta jump over the net.
Kinya move it?
Lemme'ave a look
We can drive'im over.
Now let's getcha up.

exercise **6** Listen to the reductions in the following conversation. Write the long forms in the blanks. You may want to repeat the sentences for pronunciation practice.

NORIKO: I triedta call you this morning. I heardja had an accident. Are you okay?

DEBBIE: Yeah, but my brother hurt his foot. I'll have to drive'im to school for a while.

NORIKO: That's too bad. Say! Kinya lemme'ave a ride, too?

PART **two** *Summarizing Main Ideas, page 61*

exercise **1** You will hear a radio report about an earthquake. Discuss with a partner what kinds of information the report will probably give you. Then listen to the report.

NEWSCASTER: There was a major earthquake in central Guatemala today. A seven on the Richter scale, it was the strongest earthquake there in twenty years. Reports indicate that more than eight hundred people died and thousands more were injured. The earthquake occurred near the city of Puebla, where damage to buildings was extensive.

exercise 2   Listen to the report again. Make up four questions about the earthquake report. Use the question words below.

PART **three**   *Guessing Information, page 62*

Focus on Testing

Listen to the following conversations about emergencies. Decide what each situation is, and circle the answer in your book. Then listen to the next part of the conversation, which gives you the correct answer to the previous question.

A: When the lights went out, it was really coming down outside. Then the wind started up, and all the windows sharted to shake so hard that I thought the house was going to fall down.
B: Then what happened?
A: I looked out the window and saw the sky covered with those dangerous, dark clouds.

1. The situation is probably . . .

A: It was the worst storm last year.

A: He is lying on the floor.
B: What color is his face?
A: He's blue and perspiring. He says he has chest pains. Please hurry!

2. This situation is probably . . .

B: It's probably a heart attack. Don't move him. We'll be right out.

A: Oh, no! I don't have a spare!
B: Well, we certainly can't drive into town this way. We'll have to change it.
A: I guess I'll try to find a phone. I'll call a service station so that they can tow the car into town.

3. This conversation is about . . .

A: I don't believe this! My second flat tire this week!

A: Take a look at the map. I'm sure we can figure out our position.
B: I've been looking around for a few minutes, but nothing looks familiar.
A: I think we got off at the wrong bus stop.

4. In this conversation . . .

B: So we really are lost, huh?

(TV NEWS BROADCAST): There was more rain today in the Midwest. This makes the third day of heavy rainfall. Many people in cities near the Mississippi River are leaving their homes. They are afraid that water from the rain-filled river is going to destroy their homes. Last night, one family near St. Louis,

Missouri reported over two feet of water in their home. More rain is expected for tomorrow.

5. The situation is . . .

A flood emergency now exists in much of the Midwest.

PART **four** *Listening Tasks, page 62*

activity 1

Herb goes to a clinic for his knee. In the waiting room he overhears a police officer talking to a woman and her companion. Listen to what they tell the police officer.

POLICE OFFICER: So a man took your purse. What did he look like?
WOMAN: Well, he was a young white man.
MAN: Yeah. I'd say about twenty-five. And he was tall, over six feet, I'm sure. And he was very thin.
POLICE OFFICER: What was he wearing?
WOMAN: Blue jeans and some kind of a jacket.
POLICE OFFICER: What color?
WOMAN: Brown.
MAN: No, it wasn't. It was red.
WOMAN: Was it? I don't remember. I'm so upset.
POLICE OFFICER: What else can you tell me? How about his hair?
WOMAN: I couldn't see his hair because he had a hat on.
MAN: I think he had short blond hair and he was wearing sunglasses.
POLICE OFFICER: Did he have a beard or a mustache?
WOMAN: No.
POLICE OFFICER: Did you see any unusual marks? ·
WOMAN: What do you mean?
POLICE OFFICER: You know, a cut on his face, a tattoo, or something?
WOMAN: Ah . . .
MAN: Oh, yeah, yeah, he had a tattoo—a tattoo of a bird on his hand.
WOMAN: Well, I didn't see that. I was too nervous.
POLICE OFFICER: Do you remember anything else?
MAN: No, I don't think so.
POLICE OFFICER: Well if you do, please call us.

activity 2

Listen again. Complete the form with a description of the thief.

activity 4

Choking is a common emergency. Listen to the following instructions; they tell how to help someone who is choking. Circle (a) or (b) to match each instruction with the correct picture.

1. Ask him if he can speak.
2. If he cannot speak, stand behind him.
3. Put your arms around his stomach and make a fist.
4. Push your fist into his stomach and pull up hard at the same time. Quickly do this three times.

CHAPTER **seven**

Health

PART **one**   *Listening to Conversations, page 70*

Getting the Main Idea

exercise 1   Peter and Kenji want to get in shape. They are thinking about joining a health club. Close your book and listen to their conversation. You may not understand every word. Listen for the main ideas.

INSTRUCTOR:	I think you're going to like it here. Let me show you around. Here's the weight room. Our instructors can show you how to use these machines.
PETER:	That looks great, doesn't it?
KENJI:	Yeah.
INSTRUCTOR:	And here is our aerobics class . . .
KENJI:	Is this class for beginners?
INSTRUCTOR:	Well, it looks like it, doesn't it? It's called "low impact," but they're really working harder than you think.
PETER:	So that's pretty good for your heart . . .
INSTRUCTOR:	It sure is. But you should do it at least three times a week if you want to be in good shape.
KENJI:	There are better ways to get in shape, aren't there?
INSTRUCTOR:	Well, some people prefer swimming. Let me show you our pool . . .
PETER:	Wow! Look at that woman in the middle lane. She's really fast!
INSTRUCTOR:	Oh, yeah. That's Ellen, one of our instructors.
KENJI:	I'd like to take lessons from *her*!
INSTRUCTOR:	You're not the only one. C'mon, I'll show you the showers and the locker room. You know, you ought to join the club before the end of the month.
KENJI:	Really? Why?
INSTRUCTOR:	Because we have a special discount for students this month. Let's go to my office. I'll tell you all about it.

exercise 2   Now you will hear seven questions about the conversation. Listen to the questions. Then write answers to the questions on the lines below. Discuss your answers with your classmates.

1. What were Peter and Kenji doing in the health club?
2. What did they think of the weight room?
3. What other things did they see at the club?
4. What kind of exercise class did they see?
5. What's another exercise some people prefer?
6. Who was the fast swimmer in the pool?
7. Why should Peter and Kenji join the club this month?

Stress, page 71

exercise 3

Listen to the first part of the conversation again. Repeat each sentence during the pause. Then fill in the missing stressed words.

INSTRUCTOR: I think you're going to like it here. Let me show you around. Here's the weight room. Our instructors can show you how to use these machines.

PETER: That looks great, doesn't it?

KENJI: Yeah.

INSTRUCTOR: And here is our aerobics class . . .

KENJI: Is this class for beginners?

INSTRUCTOR: Well, it looks like it, doesn't it? It's called "low impact," but they're really working harder than you think.

PETER: So that's pretty good for your heart . . .

INSTRUCTOR: It sure is. But you should do it at least three times a week if you want to be in good shape.

exercise 4

Now listen to the rest of the conversation. Mark the stressed words.

KENJI: There are better ways to get in shape, aren't there?

INSTRUCTOR: Well, some people prefer swimming. Let me show you our pool . . .

PETER: Wow! Look at that woman in the middle lane. She's really fast!

INSTRUCTOR: Oh, yeah. That's Ellen, one of our instructors.

KENJI: I'd like to take lessons from *her*!

INSTRUCTOR: You're not the only one. C'mon, I'll show you the showers and the locker room. You know, you ought to join the club before the end of the month.

KENJI: Really? Why?

INSTRUCTOR: Because we have a special discount for students this month. Let's go to my office. I'll tell you all about it.

Intonation with Tag Questions, page 72

Questions at the end of sentences are called tag questions. Affirmative statements take negative tag questions: He is strong, isn't he? Negative statements take affirmative tag questions: She isn't tired, is she? People use tag questions in two ways. Listen to the following examples. Notice the difference in intonation.

1.   Your father is a doctor, isn't he?↑

2.   Your father is a doctor, isn't he?↓

In the first example, the speaker is unsure of the answer. His voice goes up: Your father is a doctor, isn't he?↑ In the second example, the speaker is almost sure the father is a doctor. His voice goes down: Your father is a doctor, isn't he?↓

exercise 5

1.   Repeat the first five sentences on the tape. As in the first example, the voice goes up at the end of the tag question.

We need our tennis shoes, don't we?
The pool is warm, isn't it?
You play football, don't you?
You don't smoke, do you?
You didn't hurt yourself, did you?

2. Now repeat the next five sentences. As in the second example, the voice goes down at the end of the tag question.

My father looks healthy, doesn't he?
It's a difficult exercise, isn't it?
Those people love to dance, don't they?
She can swim fast, can't she?
Exercise helps your heart, doesn't it?

exercise **6**   Now listen to the examples from the dialogue. From the intonation, decide if the speaker was sure or unsure of the answer. Circle the correct answer.

1. That looks great, doesn't it?
2. Well, it looks like it, doesn't it?
3. That's very good for your heart, isn't it?
4. There are better ways to get in shape, aren't there?

PART **two**   *Summarizing Main Ideas, page 73*

exercise **1**   Barbara is at the university health service. Listen to her conversation with her doctor.

DOCTOR: Oh, it's you again! What seems to be the trouble?
BARBARA: Well, I woke up this morning with a terrible headache.
DOCTOR: Yes?
BARBARA: And my stomach was upset too. I'm feeling really weak, and my whole body feels hot, and my muscles hurt. Oh, and I'm starting to get a sore throat.
DOCTOR: Well, your forehead feels really warm. You probably have a fever. Let me see your throat.
BARBARA: Ahhhh.
DOCTOR: Ah-hah. It's all red and swollen. I think you've got another case of the flu. You were sick just last month, weren't you?
BARBARA: Yeah, I was.
DOCTOR: Are you taking good care of yourself?
BARBARA: What do you mean?
DOCTOR: Well, do you eat right and do you get enough sleep?
BARBARA: I think so. . . . Well, right now I'm studying for some tests and I'm very tired.
DOCTOR: I want you to take two aspirins four times a day, drink a lot of juice, and get plenty of rest. If your throat doesn't get better in a week, I want you to call me, okay?
BARBARA: So I don't need a prescription?
DOCTOR: Not yet. Well, take care of yourself, and don't work too hard.

exercise **2**   Listen to the conversation again and take notes. The first one is done as an example.

Focus on Testing

exercise **1**

Listen to each conversation. There is one "strange," or unusual, thing in each. Say what it is. Then listen to the next part of the conversation. It gives you the correct answer.

CONVERSATION 1

A: Hello, may I take your order?
B: Yes, I'd like a lettuce salad with low-fat cottage cheese; no dressing, please. One slice of toast, no butter.
A: Anything to drink?
B: Do you have sugar-free cola?
A: Yes, we do. Will that be all, miss?
B: Yes. . . . Oh, wait! For dessert I'll have a piece of chocolate cake with ice cream.

    1. What's strange about this conversation?

A: Gee. Before you ordered that cake, I thought you were on a diet.

CONVERSATION 2

A: So, that was a good workout, wasn't it?
B: Yeah. Let's see . . . What did we do? We ran three miles, we played some tennis, and we did 50 sit-ups.
A: Yeah. Let's get a drink of water.
B: Wait! Let me go get my cigarettes. They're in the car.

    2. What's strange about this conversation?

A: You know, you take such good care of yourself and get so much exercise. I really don't understand why you smoke.

CONVERSATION 3

A: Ouch, don't touch my back. My skin is really burning.
B: Your whole body is getting red, you know. You should be careful.
A: Yeah, I guess so.
B: How much longer are we going to stay out here?
A: Oh, another hour at least. I just love this beach.

    3. What's strange about this conversation?

B: You shouldn't lie in the sun so long without protection. Can't you see the sunburn?

exercise **2**

Listen to the following dialogues. What are they about? Circle the correct answer.

CONVERSATION 1

A: So Nancy went into the hospital last night?
B: Yes, her husband is waiting for the news now.
A: Is this her first?
B: Yes, so they're both very nervous. Especially Steve.

A: When can Nancy come home?
B: If all goes well, they'll both be home in two days. It's exciting, isn't it?

   1. The situation is . . .

A: Yes, having your first baby is always very special.

CONVERSATION 2

A: These carrots are completely natural.
B: What about your eggs? Are they fresh?
A: Of course. All our eggs come from local farms daily.
B: You sell vitamins, don't you?
A: Yes, they're right next to the nuts over there.
B: Your stuff looks great but a little expensive.
A: Well, we sell only the best.

   2. The speakers are in a . . .

B: Well, I guess this is the best health food store in town.

PART four *Listening Tasks, page 75*

activity

You will hear three telephone conversations about health situations. Take notes on each call.

CONVERSATION 1

A: University Dental Clinic. May I help you?
B: Yes, I'd like to make an appointment.
A: Do you have a problem, or is it just for a checkup?
B: I think I broke a tooth.
A: Well, can you come in tomorrow morning?
B: No, but how about after lunch?
A: Well, let me see . . . Dr. Jones can probably take you at around two o'clock. How's that?
B: That's great. Where is your office?
A: We're at 532 Western Avenue. That's near Third Street.
B: Okay. I'll see you tomorrow at two.

CONVERSATION 2

A: Drugs R Us. May I help you?
B: Yes, I'd like to know if my prescription is ready.
A: What's the name, please?
B: Ellen Beattie.
A: Spell that, please.
B: B-E-A-T-T-I-E.
A: Oh, yes, here it is. It comes to $14.95.
B: Are there any special instructions?
A: Well, let me see. Take the pills every six hours with food. Don't mix them with alcohol. But don't worry. The instructions are also on the bottle.
B: Okay. How late can I pick it up?
A: Today we're only open until five o'clock.
B: All right. Thanks a lot. I'll be in later.

CONVERSATION 3

A: Family Medicine.

B: Hi, Sherry. This is Penny Berkowitz.

A: Hi. You're bringing your baby in this afternoon, aren't you?

B: Well, our car broke down. So I'd like to change our appointment with Dr. Stork, if that's okay.

A: Sure. What's a good time for you?

B: Can I come in on Monday?

A: How about ten o'clock?

B: Fine.

A: Okay. We'll see you then.

B: Oh, while we're on the phone, my husband needs a checkup. Can you take him one evening next week?

A: I think so. What about Tuesday at six o'clock with Dr. Miller?

B: That's perfect. Thanks. Bye-bye.

CHAPTER eight

Entertainment and the Media

PART one *Listening to Conversations, page 80*

Getting the Main Idea

exercise 1

Barbara and Marsha are talking about television and newpapers. They don't exactly agree. Close your book and listen to their conversation. You may not understand every word. Listen for the main ideas.

BARBARA: Hey, listen to this! The average American family watches six hours of TV a day.

MARSHA: A day! You're joking.

BARBARA: No, it says so right here in this magazine.

MARSHA: I guess I'm not an average American. I usually don't watch TV at all. Most of the programs are terrible.

BARBARA: Well, some of the programs are bad, but a lot are okay. And what about the sports and news?

MARSHA: Well, yeah, I guess sports are okay. But for news, I prefer a good newspaper.

BARBARA: Why do you say that?

MARSHA: Well, I hate all those commercials, and the TV news stories never tell you very much. A newspaper has more information, and you can read just what you want to.

BARBARA: Yeah, I see what you mean.

MARSHA: Hey, look at this.

BARBARA: What?

MARSHA: There's an article here about a TV mystery that sounds interesting.

BARBARA: Don't tell me you want to watch TV!

MARSHA: Well, it *is* Sherlock Holmes. Can I stay here to watch it?

BARBARA: Sure. But be careful, or you'll turn into an "average American."

exercise 2

Now you will hear six questions about the conversation. Listen to the questions. Then write answers to the questions on the lines below. Discuss your answers with your classmates.

1. How much TV does the average American family watch?
2. Why doesn't Marsha usually watch TV?
3. What does Barbara think?
4. Why doesn't Marsha like news on TV?
5. Why does Marsha prefer newspapers for news?
6. Why does Marsha want to stay at Barbara's house?

Stress, page 81

exercise 3   Listen to the first part of the conversation again. Repeat each sentence during the pause. Then fill in the missing stressed words.

BARBARA: Hey, listen to this! The average American family watches six hours of TV a day.

MARSHA: A day! You're joking.

BARBARA: No, it says so right here in this magazine.

MARSHA: I guess I'm not an average American. I usually don't watch TV at all. Most of the programs are terrible.

BARBARA: Well, some of the programs are bad, but a lot are okay. And what about the sports and news?

MARSHA: Well, yeah, I guess sports are okay. But for news, I prefer a good newspaper.

BARBARA: Why do you say that?

MARSHA: Well, I hate all those commercials, and the TV news stories never tell you very much. A newspaper has more information, and you can read just what you want to.

BARBARA: Yeah, I see what you mean.

exercise 4   Now listen to the rest of the conversation. Take notes, writing down key words (which are usually the stressed words) as in the following examples. Don't try to copy whole sentences. Then re-create the conversation with a partner, using your notes as a guide.

MARSHA: Hey, look at this.

BARBARA: What?

MARSHA: There's an article here about a TV mystery that sounds interesting.

BARBARA: Don't tell me you want to watch TV!

MARSHA: Well, it *is* Sherlock Holmes. Can I stay here to watch it?

BARBARA: Sure. But be careful, or you'll turn into an "average American."

PART two   *Summarizing Main Ideas, page 82*

exercise 2   Now listen to the report and check your predictions.

RADIO ANNOUNCER: Good evening. Our top story tonight: A small airplane carrying six people landed safely in traffic on Highway One. Two of the passengers received minor back injuries and one of the passengers suffered a broken leg. Here's reporter Larry Jones at the scene of the landing.

REPORTER: Good evening, Mark. I'm standing here with two drivers who almost hit the plane as it landed. Could you tell me what you thought as you watched the plane coming down?

WITNESS A: Well, at first I wasn't scared. But then I saw it was flying very low. So I drove off the road in a hurry.

WITNESS B: I almost didn't see the plane at all. It happened so fast. When I finally heard the plane's motor, I knew something was wrong. And I hit my brakes. Phew . . . it was really close. I'm still shaking.

REPORTER: Fortunately no one on the ground was hurt, but the plane blocked the road for over an hour. Captain John McNamara of the local highway police thinks the plane ran out of gasoline. A complete investigation will begin tomorrow. Back to you, Mark.

exercise 3   Listen to the news report again and take notes.

PART three   *Guessing Information, page 83*

Focus on Testing

Listen to the following commercials. Circle the letter of the product being advertised in each one. Then listen to the next part of the commerical. It contains the correct answer.

RADIO ANN: Looking for a healthy start and good taste? No time for bacon and eggs? Pick up your morning with a bowl of Flakos!

1. What are Flakos?

A: Hello?
B: Hi, Marge. Are you asleep?
A: Not anymore. Who is this?
B: It's Bill. I'm out in California.
A: It's two o'clock in the morning.
B: Yeah, but you know how cheap it is to call at night? I'm saving a lot of money with Fonos' new low rates!

2. This is an ad for a . . .

RADIO ANN: Fonos, the phone company that saves you money all day—and all night!

Hi! This is Tex Lewis. I'll do anything to sell you one of these fine beauties. Lookie here. We've got a 1994 sedan here, with low mileage, automatic transmission. This baby is clean; got new tires and new paint. Take a test drive today. And it can be yours for just $12,000, or $500 per month. Come in and check it out. See you soon.

3. This is an ad for . . .

RADIO ANN: Tex's Used Cars. Quality cars for less.

A: Honey, make me a sandwich.
B: Henry! It's two o'clock in the morning. I'm tired.
A: Honey, what's on TV?
B: I don't know. It's three o'clock in the morning.
A: Honey, can I have some breakfast?
B: Henry, it's four o'clock in the morning. Why don't you take some Dreamease?

4. Dreamease is a . . .

RADIO ANN: Dreamease, the nighttime sleep aid that helps you get the rest you need.

WOMAN: I can't tell you, Rob. I just can't.
MAN: Don't treat me this way, Daisy. I need you and you know it.
RADIO ANNOUNCER: Her secret can destroy a life. Will she tell it? Find out this Monday at nine on KLA.

5. This is an ad for . . .

RADIO ANN: "Daisy," the most popular drama on television.

activity **2**   Now listen to their conversation. Each time you hear a pause, fill in the missing information. Go over your answers with a group of classmates.

MARSHA: What's on TV tonight?

RAUL: What time is it now?

MARSHA: It's almost seven-thirty.

RAUL: Are there any game shows on now?

MARSHA: Yeah, at seven-thirty, there's one called "Family Fight" on Channel 4.

RAUL: "Family Fight" is a really stupid show.

MARSHA: Are there any good movies on?

RAUL: Well, there are three movies on at eight o'clock. But I'm not sure if they're interesting or not.

MARSHA: Really? Which ones are they?

RAUL: There's *The Music Man* on Channel 13—you know, that musical comedy.

MARSHA: Nah!

RAUL: Then on Channel 3 there's *Red River*. It's a western with John Wayne.

MARSHA: Ugh. I hate westerns.

RAUL: And then there's the movie *Mr. Smith Goes to Washington*. I hear it's very funny . . . That's on Channel 7.

MARSHA: Oh, wait—what's tonight? Wednesday? Great! My favorite comedy series is on at nine o'clock.

RAUL: At nine? You must be kidding—you don't want to watch that show "Happy Days?" Channel 5 should take it off, it's so dumb.

MARSHA: "Happy Days" is not dumb. It's fun.

MARSHA: So what do you want to watch from seven-thirty to nine o'clock?

RAUL: Let me see if there are any sports . . . Great, there's a tennis match on Channel 11 from eight to nine.

MARSHA: Tennis? But you watched tennis at the club all afternoon.

RAUL: So, I love tennis.

RAUL: Anyway, the news is coming on at eight-thirty. Want to watch it?

MARSHA: Okay. But let's not watch Channel 9. Their reporters are boring.

RAUL: They sure are. Channel 2 has much better news reporters.

MARSHA: Channel 2? But the new guy on Channel 4 is so good-looking.

CHAPTER **nine**

Social Life

PART one   *Listening to Conversations, page 88*

Getting the Main Idea

exercise 1   Herb is visiting his hometown in Texas. He runs into two old friends on the street. Close your book and listen to their conversation. You may not understand every word. Listen for the main ideas.

SALLY: Yolanda, I can't believe it! Look! It's Herb Myers. How are you?

HERB: Sally? Yolanda? Wow! I haven't seen you guys in ages!

YOLANDA: I know. You look great!

HERB: Thanks! You too.

YOLANDA: So what have you been up to?

HERB: Lots of things. I'm at Faber College now.

SALLY: Really? That's great!

HERB: Yeah, I've been studying pretty hard so far.

YOLANDA: Sure you have . . .

SALLY: What's your major—tennis?

HERB: No, it's . . uh . . actually, computer science. Anyway, what have *you* guys been up to all year?

YOLANDA: Well, I got married, and I have a baby boy now.

HERB: No kidding! Congratulations! And how about you, Sally? You're not married too, are you?

SALLY: No way! I've been too busy with my new job selling computers. They've been sending me all over the country this past year. I just love it.

HERB: That's terrific. You'll have to tell me all about it. Say, you haven't seen Carl Walters around, have you? What's *he* been doing lately?

YOLANDA: Well, actually I saw him this morning. He's my husband.

exercise 2   Now you will hear five questions about the conversation. Listen to the questions. Then write answers to the questions on the lines below. Discuss your answers with your classmates.

1. When was the last time Herb probably saw Sally and Yolanda?
2. Herb says he's been studying hard. What do the girls think?
3. Yolanda got married last year. What has Sally been doing this past year?
4. Why does Sally like her job?
5. Why was Herb probably surprised at the end of the conversation?

Stress, page 89

exercise 3   Listen to the first part of the conversation again. Repeat each sentence during the pause. Then fill in the missing stressed words.

SALLY: Yolanda, I can't believe it! Look! It's Herb Myers. How are you?

HERB: Sally? Yolanda? Wow! I haven't seen you guys in ages!

YOLANDA: I know. You look great!

HERB: Thanks! You too.

YOLANDA: So what have you been up to?

HERB: Lots of things. I'm at Faber College now.

SALLY: Really? That's great!

HERB: Yeah, I've been studying pretty hard so far.

YOLANDA: Sure you have . . .

SALLY: What's your major—tennis?

HERB: No, it's . . uh . . actually, computer science. Anyway, what have *you* guys been up to all year?

exercise 4   Now listen to the rest of the conversation. Take notes, writing down key words as in the example. Don't try to copy whole sentences. Afterward, re-create the conversation with a partner, using your notes as a guide.

YOLANDA: Well, I got married and I have a baby boy now.

HERB: No kidding! Congratulations! And how about you, Sally? You're not married too, are you?

SALLY: No way! I've been too busy with my new job selling computers. They've been sending me all over the country this past year. I just love it.

HERB: That's terrific. You'll have to tell me all about it. Say, you haven't seen Carl Walters around, have you? What's *he* been doing lately?

YOLANDA: Well, actually I saw him this morning. He's my husband.

Intonation with Exclamations, page 90

To express strong feelings (surprise, anger, happiness), we use exclamations. These are expressions that we pronounce with especially strong emphasis and with falling intonation at the end.

examples: Wow!   I can't believe it!
That's great!   That's awful!

exercise 5   Repeat the following exclamations from the dialogue. Follow the stress and intonation patterns carefully.

Yolanda, I can't believe it!
Look!
Wow! I haven't seen you guys in ages!
You look great!
That's great!
No kidding!
Congratulations!
No way!
That's terrific!

exercise 6   Now listen to some statements and questions on the tape. During the pause, respond with an exclamation. Use a different exclamation each time.

example: You hear: I just got six hundred on my TOEFL test.
You say: That's great!

You will hear six speakers.

1: Guess what? I'm getting married next month.
2: My sister just had triplets.
3: Would you like a job for a dollar an hour?
4: I've been exercising a lot and have lost all that extra weight.
5: Someone hit my car yesterday. It's going to cost $1,000 to repair.
6: I met the President of the United States yesterday.

PART **two** *Summarizing Main Ideas, page 91*

exercise 1   Listen as Sally tries to arrange a "blind date" for her friend Beverly. A blind date is an arranged date between two people who don't know each other.

SALLY: Listen, a friend of mine is coming to town next week. I think you might like him.
BEVERLY: Well, I really don't like blind dates. But tell me about him anyway.
SALLY: Well, he *is* very good-looking.
BEVERLY: Oh, yeah? Tell me more.
SALLY: He's got dark hair and green eyes and a wonderful smile. He had a beard the last time I saw him. He has his own business.
BEVERLY: That's nice. What kind of business?
SALLY: Import/export. And he loves to travel.
BEVERLY: About how old is he?
SALLY: He's almost thirty.
BEVERLY: Does he like dancing or music?
SALLY: He loves jazz, and he's played the piano for years. I'm sure he likes dancing too.
BEVERLY: Wow, he sounds great! Maybe he could come to a football game next weekend.
SALLY: Oh, I don't know if Franco would like that.
BEVERLY: Why is that?
SALLY: Well, they don't play American football in Italy. They play soccer.
BEVERLY: Italy? You mean he's Italian?
SALLY: Yes. So there is one small problem, I guess.
BEVERLY: Don't tell me . . .
SALLY: Right. He doesn't speak English.

exercise 2   Listen again and take notes about Franco.

exercise 4   You'll hear a brief lecture on American football. What do you know about this sport? Have you ever seen an American football game? What do the players look like? As you listen, you might try to compare it to football or soccer in your home country.

For a long time, baseball was the most popular sport in the United States. But now, football is probably the most popular sport. It is also popular in Canada.

In the fall, students in high schools and colleges and professional players all over the country play football. Football players wear strange-looking uniforms to protect them because it is a rough game, which can be dangerous.

The object, or goal, of the game is to carry the football from one end of the field to the other. Players can run with the ball, throw it, or sometimes even kick it to score points.

Most good high school football players can enter an American university easily. The best college football players often become professional players. Many professional players are rich and famous, but they usually don't play for more than six or eight years.

Football might be hard for most people to play, but it's certainly fun to watch. From September through January, people all over the country spend weekends and Monday nights in front of the TV set. In January every year, the two best American football teams play each other in the Super Bowl to see which team is the best. Millions of people around the world watch this championship game on TV.

exercise **5**   Listen to the talk again and take notes.

PART **three**   *Guessing Information, page 92*

Focus on Testing

Listen to the following conversations from Larry's party. Circle the sentence that best describes each conversation. Then listen to the next part. It gives you the correct answer.

CONVERSATION 1

MAN: So how long have you lived here?
WOMAN: I've lived here all my life. It's a fun town.
MAN: Yeah, I'm starting to see that. Maybe you can show me some of your favorite places sometime. I still don't really know a lot of the best things to do here.

Which of these sentences is true?

WOMAN: Sure. How long have you been in town?
MAN: Only about three months.

CONVERSATION TWO

MAN: I'm glad I left. The pay wasn't great, as you know, and the office manager was a pain in the neck.
WOMAN: He still is. Every day I hate going to work. But it's hard to find a better job.

Which of these sentences is true?

MAN: I really enjoyed working with you, of course. I just hated the boss.

CONVERSATION THREE

MAN: So maybe we can have lunch sometime?
WOMAN: Well, it's difficult for me to get away from work. I'm very busy.
MAN: Well, how about dinner?
WOMAN: Gee, I'm usually too tired to go out after work.
MAN: Can I call you over the weekend?
WOMAN: Well, this weekend my friend is coming from Miami, and I'll probably be out most of the time.

Which of these sentences is true?

WOMAN: Actually, he's my boyfriend, so I really can't go out with you.

CONVERSATION FOUR

WOMAN: Where's Tony?

MAN: At the bar, of course.

WOMAN: That's his fourth Scotch tonight, isn't it?

MAN: I don't know. Why do you ask?

WOMAN: Don't you remember last weekend? We had to carry him home.

Which of these sentences is true?

WOMAN: Tony's drinking really worries me.

CONVERSATION FIVE

WOMAN: I waited forty-five minutes before I left for the party.

MAN: I thought you were going to pick me up. I had to take a taxi.

WOMAN: Wait a minute. You said you wanted to leave your car at my house.

MAN: I didn't say that. I said I wanted to leave my car at home.

Which of these sentences is true?

WOMAN: Listen, I'm sorry. Let's not fight over this misunderstanding, okay?

PART four *Listening Tasks, page 93*

activity

Sally and Herb plan to go out over the weekend. Sally's making a few telephone calls to get some information. Think about what kind of information she needs from (1) a movie theater, (2) a nightclub, and (3) a friend giving a party. Listen to each call and take notes.

CALL 1

Hello. This is the Fox Theater, located in the Town and Country Shopping Center. Today we're proud to present *Love Affair* with Warren Beatty and Annette Bening. Show times for Saturday are two, six, and ten o'clock. Tickets are $8, $4.50 for students. For more information, call 555-0832.

CALL 2

MANAGER: Hello. Jerry's Jazz Club.

SALLY: Hi. I'd like some information.

MANAGER: Yes, what would you like to know?

SALLY: First, is there any live music tonight?

MANAGER: Yes, we have a Brazilian singer. There are shows at nine and eleven.

SALLY: How much is the show?.

MANAGER: We have a $10 cover charge. But if you come for dinner, the show is free.

SALLY: What's your menu like?

MANAGER: Our specialty is Italian food, but we serve salads and hamburgers too.

SALLY: Fine. I'd like a reservation for two for Friday night for dinner at eight, and we'll stay for the 9 o'clock show.

CALL 3

LARRY: Hello.

SALLY: Hi, Larry? This is Sally.

LARRY: Oh, hi. Are you coming to my party Saturday night?

SALLY: Yeah. That's why I'm calling. I forgot your address.

LARRY: Oh, I'm at 825 Spring Street.

SALLY: Where's that?

LARRY: I'm three blocks west of the Town and Country Shopping Center.

SALLY: Oh, okay. What time should I come?

LARRY: Any time after eight.

SALLY: Should I bring anything?

LARRY: Just some beer or wine if you want to.

SALLY: Oh, by the way, can I bring a friend? You might even know him—Herb Myers.

LARRY: I think I do know him. Sure, bring him along.

SALLY: Great. See you then.

CHAPTER ten

Customs, Celebrations, and Holidays

Getting the Main Idea

exercise 1

Kenji is dating an American girl he met in class. He wants to buy her a gift for Valentine's Day to show her that he really likes her. Close your book and listen to the conversation between Kenji and the gift shop clerk. You may not understand every word. Listen for the main ideas.

CLERK: Yes, can I help you with anything?

KENJI: I'm looking for a Valentine's gift for my girlfriend. Well, actually, she's not my girlfriend yet, so I really don't know what to get her.

CLERK: How about some chocolate?

KENJI: Well, I think she's on a diet.

CLERK: Hmm, then how about some jewelry?

KENJI: Gosh, I really can't spend too much money.

CLERK: Okay. Let's see . . . What else? . . . Well, here's a nice bottle of cologne. I'm sure she'll like that.

KENJI: Oh, I don't know. I wanted to give her something unusual.

CLERK: I'm afraid something unusual might be expensive. Try sending her a nice card, and you can also buy her a rose. Most women like to get flowers.

KENJI: Okay. I guess that's what I'll do.

CLERK: Don't worry. I'm sure she'll like whatever you get her.

KENJI: Oh, I hope so.

exercise 2

Now you will hear five questions about the conversation. Listen to the questions. Then write answers to the questions on the lines below. Discuss your answers with your classmates.

1. What is Kenji looking for?
2. Why doesn't he want to buy any chocolate?
3. What else does the saleswoman recommend?
4. Why doesn't Kenji want to buy jewelry?
5. What does Kenji finally decide to do?

Stress, page 99

exercise 3

Listen to the first part of the conversation again. Repeat each sentence during the pause. Then fill in the missing stressed words.

CLERK: Yes, can I help you with anything?

KENJI: I'm looking for a Valentine's gift for my girlfriend. Well, actually, she's not my girlfriend yet, so I really don't know what to get her.

CLERK: How about some chocolate?

KENJI: Well, I think she's on a diet.

CLERK: Hmm, then how about some jewelry?

KENJI: Gosh, I really can't spend too much money.

exercise 4   Now listen to the rest of the conversation. Take notes, writing down key words as in the example. Don't try to copy whole sentences. Afterward, re-create the conversation with a partner, using your notes as a guide.

CLERK: Okay. Let's see . . . What else? . . . Well, here's a nice bottle of cologne. I'm sure she'll like that.

KENJI: Oh, I don't know. I wanted to give her something unusual.

CLERK: I'm afraid something unusual might be expensive. Try sending her a nice card, and you can also buy her a rose. Most women like to get flowers.

KENJI: Okay. I guess that's what I'll do.

CLERK: Don't worry. I'm sure she'll like whatever you get her.

KENJI: Oh, I hope so.

PART **two**   *Summarizing Main Ideas, page 100*

exercise 2   Now listen to the conversation, checking your predictions and trying to learn more about the holiday.

STUDENT 1: Everything is delicious, Mrs. Stevens. It really was nice of you to invite us.

MRS. S: Well, nobody should have dinner alone today. That's what Thanksgiving is all about. Is this your first Thanksgiving in the United States?

STUDENT 2: Yes. In fact, we don't really know much about it.

MRS. S: Well ask Robbie. He'll tell you all about it.

ROBBIE: Ah, come on Mom. What's this, a history lesson?

STUDENT 1: No, we're really interested. Come on, tell us.

ROBBIE: Well, see, these guys came over from Europe like maybe a thousand years ago . . .

MR. S: Not exactly. It was more like three hundred and fifty years ago.

ROBBIE: Oh, yeah, that's right. Anyway, they made good friends with the Indians, and they tried planting corn and other stuff together. But it was really hard growing all that stuff, so when they had the first harvest . . .

STUDENT 1: What's a "harvest?"

ROBBIE: You know, when they pick the food after it's done growing. So after the first harvest, the Indians and the Pilgrims had a big dinner together to thank God for their good luck.

STUDENT 2: Wait. Who were the Pilgrims?

MR. S: They were the first immigrants from Europe.

MRS. S: And the foods we are eating now are the same kinds of things that they ate.

STUDENT 1: Oh, so that's where turkey and corn and squash come from, right?

ROBBIE: Right!

STUDENT 2: But why is Thanksgiving on November 27th?

ROBBIE: It's different every year. But it's always the fourth Thursday of November. Right, Dad?

MR. S: Right. Except that in Canada they celebrate it in October.

PART **three** *Guessing Information, page 101*

Focus on Testing

Listen to the following conversations about holidays and celebrations. Decide what each situation is. Circle the best answer in your book. Then listen to the next part of the conversation. It contains the correct answer.

CONVERSATION 1

MAN: Does anyone remember the meaning of this holiday anymore?

WOMAN: Only if they watch the president talk about it on TV. Anyway, with all the picnics and the beautiful fireworks, I'm sure most people have a good time.

MAN: Boy, it sure is amazing that the United States is over two hundred years old!

What are the speakers talking about?

WOMAN: The Fourth of July is my favorite holiday, next to Christmas.

CONVERSATION 2

MAN: I think there are some more kids at the door. It's pretty late, dear. Do we have any more fruit or chocolate?

WOMAN: Of course we do.

KIDS: Trick or treat!

WOMAN: Well, what have we here? Frankenstein, Batman, and who are you?

BOY: I'm Snoopy!

WOMAN: Well, here you are.

KINDS: Thank you.

What holiday is this?

WOMAN: We gave away more candy this Halloween than last year.

CONVERSATION 3

WOMAN: You're looking younger and healthier every year.

MAN: Why, thank you. But we both know it's not true. Look at all those candles on my cake. I don't think I can blow them all out.

WOMAN: Sure you can. Oh, before I forget, here's a gift from Bob and Gail.

What are they celebrating?

MAN: Did they really remember my birthday?

CONVERSATION 4

A: So did you get a lot of presents yesterday?

B: Yeah, I got some great clothes and a CD player. How about you?

A: I got a mountain bike and a tennis racket. Did you give your parents anything special?

B: I got them tickets to a show.

A: I bet they liked that. By the way, I just heard about a great party for New Year's. Want to come?

What holiday did the speakers just celebrate?

B: Sure. Hey, do you want some Christmas cookies my mom made? They're really good.

CONVERSATION 5

A: What was she wearing?
B: It was a lovely white dress. She looked beautiful.
A: Was the ceremony at the church?
B: Not, it was at the groom's home. There were only thirty people there.
A: Where are they going to live?
B: They just bought a new house. They're moving in after their honeymoon.

What are the speakers talking about?

A: I really wanted to go to their wedding, but I couldn't.

PART **four** *Listening Tasks, page 101*

activity **2**

Now listen to the conversation. Are Mike's friends planning to do the same things that are on your list? What are they planning that's *not* on your list?

KENJI: Okay. Here's the guest list. Who wants to invite all these people? How about you, Peter?
PETER: I'll do that if you clean up the apartment first, Kenji.
KENJI: Cleaning is a woman's job. Right, Barbara?
BARBARA: Not this woman's! Anyway, I promised to bake the cake and buy the decorations. That's enough, I think.
KENJI: Okay. I'll do the cleaning then.
PETER: All right. What else do we have to do?
KENJI: What are we going to drink?
PETER: Let's get Herb to buy the beer. That will go well with his Texas chili.
BARBARA: Oh, Herb is cooking? I just love his chili.
PETER: So, what time should everyone come, Kenji?
KENJI: If everyone arrives by eight, I can bring Mike here at eight-thirty.

activity **3**

Listen again. What will each person do to prepare for the party? Briefly describe each job you hear next to the name of the person who agrees to do it.

CHAPTER eleven

Science and Technology

PART one   Listening to Conversations, page 106

Getting the Main Idea

exercise 1

Peter, Herb, Kenji, and Kenji's new girlfriend, Lisa, are discussing which parts of Faber College's new museum of science and technology they want to visit first. Close your books and listen to their conversation. You may not understand every word. Listen for the main ideas.

PETER: So where should we start? This place is huge!

LISA: Why don't we check out the transportation exhibit?

KENJI: Right! I really want to see that Maglev train that speeds along on air.

HERB: How do they do that?

LISA: Isn't it magnets that keep the train about a foot above the tracks?

KENJI: Uh huh. And there isn't any friction, so the train can reach incredible speeds.

PETER: I hear that Japan and Germany are going to have Maglev trains in service pretty soon.

HERB: Sounds interesting. But let's not miss the virtual reality lab. It's really cool. No matter where you are, you just put on a video helmet and you can be in New York—walk the streets, skate through Central Park—and you never even leave the room.

KENJI: It's probably a lot safer to see New York that way.

LISA: Maybe I'm the only one, but I'd like to see the genetic engineering wing too.

PETER: Genetic engineering? What's that about? Sounds creepy.

LISA: Well, to begin with, they've developed some new tomatoes that are supposed to be very sweet and juicy, and they don't get rotten as fast as normal tomatoes.

PETER: I don't know about that. I'm a little nervous when technology messes around with our food.

HERB: Wake up, Peter! Technology *has* been "messing around with" our food for years.

exercise 2

Now you will hear five questions about the conversation. Listen to the questions. Then write answers to the questions on the lines below. Discuss your answers with your classmates.

1. What can they see in the transportation exhibit?
2. What's so special about a Maglev train?
3. What's virtual reality?
4. What's the main advantage of the newly developed tomatoes?
5. What doesn't Peter like?

Stress, page 107

exercise 3

Now listen to the first part of the conversation again. Some of the stressed words are missing. Repeat each sentence during the pause. Then fill in the missing stressed words.

PETER: So where should we start? This place is huge!

LISA: Why don't we check out the transportation exhibit?

KENJI: Right! I really want to see that Maglev train that speeds along on air.

HERB: How do they do that?

LISA: Isn't it magnets that keep the train about a foot above the tracks?

KENJI: Uh huh. And there isn't any friction, so the train can reach incredible speeds.

PETER: I hear that Japan and Germany are going to have Maglev trains in service pretty soon.

HERB: Sounds interesting. But let's not miss the virtual reality lab. It's really cool. No matter where you are, you just put on a video helmet and you can be in New York—walk the streets, skate through Central Park—and you never even leave the room.

KENJI: It's probably a lot safer to see New York that way.

exercise 4 Now listen to the rest of the conversation. Take notes, writing down key words. Don't try to copy whole sentences. Then re-create the conversation with a partner, using your notes as a guide.

LISA: Maybe I'm the only one, but I'd like to see the genetic engineering wing too.

PETER: Genetic engineering? What's that about? Sounds creepy.

LISA: Well, to begin with, they've developed some new tomatoes that are supposed to be very sweet and juicy, and they don't get rotten as fast as normal tomatoes.

PETER: I don't know about that. I'm a little nervous when technology messes around with our food.

HERB: Wake up, Peter! Technology *has* been "messing around with" our food for years.

PART two *Summarizing Main Ideas, page 108*

exercise 1 You are going to hear someone talk about electric cars. Listen for the main ideas only. Use the space below to take notes.

Hi. My name is Dave Escobar and my neighbors think I'm crazy. In fact, my friends think so too. I just bought a car for $15,000 that can't go very fast or very far or seat more than two people. It's not fancy; no air conditioning or anything like that. Maybe you guessed it: I've bought an electric car. And you know what? I really love it.

First of all, I feel good about not using any gas and not polluting the air. You know, here in California half the air pollution is caused by cars. *Gasoline*-powered cars. We have to do something about that. Actually, Californians are already doing something. A new law says that by 1998, two percent of cars sold here must be electric. That may not sound like much, but it's a start.

Sure, my electric car isn't as convenient as my old one. For one thing, the battery runs out after about 60 miles—for me, that's about every three days. So that means I have to recharge it often. And I can't just go to any gas station like I used to. I have to find a special recharging station and leave the car there for several hours. And as I said, it's not the fastest car I've ever had. Its top speed is only about 65 miles per hour—which is okay because I only drive it around the city. One good thing, though. My electric car is quieter than gas-powered cars. So it's cutting down on *noise* pollution too.

All in all, I think electric cars are the wave of the future. I hope in a few years we'll have improved batteries, more recharge stations, and maybe even special highway lanes and parking spaces for people who drive electric cars. Then the number of people who'll buy them will increase and, for sure, the price will come down. And then we'll see if my friends and neighbors still think I'm "crazy."

Listen again and organize your notes using the outline form below. Mention only the key advantages, disadvantages, and future of electric cars. Compare your finished outline with those of your classmates. Then retell the story in your own words.

PART three *Guessing Information, page 109*

Focus on Testing

Listen to the following conversations about problems caused by machines. Decide what kinds of machines they are talking about. Compare your answers with classmates and discuss the reasons for your choices.

CONVERSATION 1

A: Why is it still so hot in here? It's been going for 30 minutes!
B: I know. I set it for 75 but it keeps turning off every time it reaches 80.
A: Hm. Let me see. The thermostat must be broken.

CONVERSATION 2

A: Has anyone called?
B: Nope. No messages.
A: Are you sure? The light is blinking. Oh no! Look . . .
B: Oh! I see. The tape is full, so nothing got recorded. Let me rewind it.

CONVERSATION 3

A: I've bought a new battery, I've bought a new starter, and I've had the wiring checked. No mechanic can find anything wrong with it.
B: Maybe there's nothing wrong with it.
A: Of course there is. I'm telling you, it won't start. It happens at least two, three times a month. I turn the key, and it just won't start.

CONVERSATION 4

A: I've paid $300 for this thing, and I can't have a decent conversation with anybody. There is so much noise, I can only hear every other sentence.
B: Have you tried changing channels?
A: Yes, I have.
B: Then your batteries must be weak.

CONVERSATION 5

A: There's a black line in the middle of the page every time I receive something. And when I send something too. My clients are complaining.
B: Are you using cheap paper?
A: No, I don't think that's it.
B: Have you tried cleaning the inside? Sometimes the roller gets dusty.
A: Yeah, maybe that's it. What should I use?
B: Just a little alcohol on a clean cloth.

CONVERSATION 6

A: What happened?

B: The screen just went blank. I think I've lost all my data.

A: Haven't you been backing up your work? I told you to save everything frequently, at least every ten minutes.

B: I know, I know. How could this happen?

A: I think your hard drive just crashed. Or maybe it was a power surge. Let's turn it back on again and see.

PART four *Listening Tasks, page 110*

activity 2

Look at the illustration below as you listen to Lisa explain how to set a VCR clock. The picture shows the buttons on the VCR. Listen carefully to Lisa's instructions. For each step she describes, write the step number over the button or buttons Peter should push.

LISA: I'm surprised at you, Peter. Really, this stuff's not too hard.

PETER: Yeah, well . . . I hate reading instruction manuals.

LISA: I see. Well, anyway, it says here that first you have to press the clock set button.

PETER: Let me see. That's the large one over on the left, isn't it?

LISA: Yeah, the one at the bottom left.

PETER: How's that?

LISA: Good. Next we've got to set the day of the week.

PETER: Well, today's Friday. How do I make it say Friday?

LISA: It says to press a numeric key corresponding to the day of the week.

PETER: So here's Friday right under number six, so let's press six.

LISA: Fine.

PETER: But why is Friday flashing on and off?

LISA: It's not really set yet. You have to press the enter key.

PETER: Oh, O.K. So that's um . . .

LISA: Below the numbered keys on the bottom.

PETER: Got it! You know I can't read these very easily without my glasses.

LISA: Uh huh. So now what, professor?

PETER: I guess it's time to set the time.

LISA: You got it.

PETER: My watch says it's 7:29 so I press the seven, and then . . .

LISA: Not so fast. First you need to press the AM/PM key for the correct half of the day.

PETER: Oh, I see. Here it is. P . . . M . . . Cool. Now I suppose I have to hit enter again.

LISA: Not yet, actually. First you input the time.

PETER: Fine. I've got 7:30 exactly so I'll hit seven . . . three . . . and zero.

LISA: Good. Now don't forget to hit enter or the time will be canceled in about four seconds.

PETER: Entered! Wow. My VCR actually says Friday, 7:30 PM and I did it myself!

LISA: Give me a break. You're lucky I'm not taping this conversation for your science professors.

PETER: Don't even think about it!

CHAPTER **twelve**

You, the Consumer

<u>PART**one**</u> *Listening to Conversations, page 114*

Getting the Main Idea

exercise 1

Marsha is shopping in a large department store. Close your books and listen to this conversation between Marsha, a salesclerk, and another customer. You may not understand every word. Listen for the main ideas.

MAN:	Miss! Could I please get some help here?
SALESWOMAN:	Certainly, sir. I'll be right there.
MARSHA:	I believe I was here first.
SALESWOMAN:	All right. What can I help you with?
MARSHA:	I'm interested in those ties in that case.
MAN:	I'd like to see those ties.
SALESWOMAN:	Well, that makes it easy. Why don't you both take a look at what we've got. These are our designer ties, and they're $50 each.
MARSHA:	Are they all silk?
SALESWOMAN:	Uh-huh.
MAN:	Oh, I think I like this striped one in blue.
MARSHA:	Wow, that's really gorgeous. It would look terrific on you.
MAN:	Yeah?
MARSHA:	Yeah. I mean it goes so well with your eyes. I really *like* it. In fact, I think I'll buy one myself.
MAN:	Well, I will too.
SALESWOMAN:	I hate to disappoint you, but that's the last one left.
MARSHA:	Oh, really?
MAN:	Oh, no . . . Well, I'll tell you what: *You* can have the tie, if you join me for a cup of coffee.
MARSHA:	Hmmm. Well, I really can't have coffee, but my boyfriend would sure love that tie.

exercise 2

Now you will hear five questions about the conversation. Listen to the questions. Then write answers to the questions on the lines below. Discuss your answers with your classmates.

1. Who is interested in buying some ties?
2. Who was first in line?
3. Which tie do they both like?
4. Why can't they both buy the same kind of tie?
5. How do you know that the man likes Marsha?

Stress, page 115

exercise 3   Now listen to the first part of the conversation again. Some of the stressed words are missing. Repeat each sentence during the pause. Then fill in the missing stressed words.

MAN: Miss! Could I please get some help here?

SALESWOMAN: Certainly, sir. I'll be right there.

MARSHA: I believe I was here first.

SALESWOMAN: All right. What can I help you with?

MARSHA: I'm interested in those ties in that case.

MAN: I'd like to see those ties.

SALESWOMAN: Well, that makes it easy. Why don't you both take a look at what we've got. These are our designer ties, and they're $50 each.

MARSHA: Are they all silk?

SALESWOMAN: Uh-huh.

MAN: Oh, I think I like this striped one in blue.

MARSHA: Wow, that's really gorgeous. It would look terrific on you.

exercise 4   Now listen to the rest of the conversation. Take notes, writing down key words. Don't try to copy whole sentences. Then re-create the conversation with a partner, using your notes as a guide.

MAN: Yeah?

MARSHA: Yeah. I mean it goes so well with your eyes. I really *like* it. In fact, I think I'll buy one myself.

MAN: Well, I will too.

SALESWOMAN: I hate to disappoint you, but that's the last one left.

MARSHA: Oh, really?

MAN: Oh, no . . . Well, I'll tell you what: *You* can have the tie, if you join me for a cup of coffee.

MARSHA: Hmmm. Well, I really can't have coffee, but my boyfriend would sure love that tie.

PART **two**   *Summarizing Main Ideas, page 116*

exercise 1   You are going to hear a radio show about how to buy a used car. Listen for the main ideas only. Use the space below to take notes.

HOST: I'm happy to have as my guest today, Steve Lewis, who's known as "Mr. Car." Good morning, Steve. Now, why would anyone want to buy a used car?

STEVE: Well, buying a used car can be tricky, but if you're careful, you can save a lot of money. You have to watch for hidden problems, but a used car is cheaper to buy and cheaper to insure than a new one.

HOST: Good point. Well, where do we start?

STEVE: First you should decide on the kind, size, and age of the car you want to buy. Smaller cars with small, efficient engines will save you hundreds of dollars a year on gas. Specialty cars, like sports cars or convertibles, will cost more to buy and repair.

HOST: Yeah, like my sister's Corvette. Now, what's the best place to find a used car?

STEVE: Well, you can try a new car dealer that also sells used cars. You might pay a little more than at a used-car dealer, but the quality of the cars is usually higher.

HOST: That's true. Of course you might also buy a used car even cheaper from a private owner. Private owners usually advertise their cars in a local newspaper. But there are some risks involved. What kind of questions should we ask a private seller, Steve?

STEVE: Well, first, is the car registered? Second, has the car ever been in an accident? And third, why is he or she selling the car? Remember, a private owner is not going to give you a warranty or guarantee to repair or replace the car. So it's important to find out about any possible problems right away. And you'll probably have to pay for the car in cash.

HOST: Right. Now, how can we avoid making the mistake of buying a car with serious problems?

STEVE: Well, you can never be 100 percent sure, but before you decide to buy, test drive the car. Then show the car to a reliable mechanic. Have the mechanic check the engine, the brakes, and other important parts.

HOST: Great advice, Steve. Thanks so much, "Mr. Car," for coming on the show.

STEVE: My pleasure.

exercise **2**   Listen again, and organize your notes using the outline form below. Mention only the key ideas. Compare your finished outline with those of your classmates.

PART **three**   *Guessing Information, page 118*

Focus on Testing

In this section, you will hear six consumer complaints. After you listen to each one, listen to the announcer's question and circle the correct answer. Then listen to the next part of the tape. It contains the correct answer to the previous question.

CONVERSATION 1

WOMAN: Hi. I just bought this here a week ago and it's already stopped working.

MAN: Oh? Was it running when you bought it?

WOMAN: Yes, although it was always a few minutes slow.

MAN: Did you check the battery?

WOMAN: Yes, I put in a new one, just to be sure.

MAN: O.K. Let me see your receipt.

What's the woman returning?

MAN: All right, we'll give you a new watch.

CONVERSATION 2

MAN: I just got my bill for this month and it's absolutely ridiculous . . .

WOMAN: Calm down, sir, and tell me what the problem is.

MAN: How can I calm down when you're asking me to pay $350? I don't even know anybody in Nicaragua or Washington, D.C. or . . .

WOMAN: Are you saying you didn't make those calls?

MAN: That's right. I want you to take these charges off my bill.

WOMAN: Tell me exactly which ones.

MAN: The ones on March 15th, 21st, and 22nd. Oh, and this one to London on the 3rd.

WOMAN: Well, sir, I'm going to fill out a form about your complaint and we will investigate these calls. A representative will call you about the results. Until then you're responsible for the rest of the charges, which come to, uh . . . $79.

What is the man upset about?

MAN: This was the biggest telephone bill I've ever received!

CONVERSATION 3

MAN: Yuk, this smells sour!
WOMAN: Well, pour it out.
MAN: I'm not going to pour it out; I'm going to take it right back to the store.
WOMAN: Do you think they'll take it back?
MAN: Sure they will. Look at the date on the carton: September 25th. And today is only the 20th. It's not supposed to be spoiled yet!

What does the man want to return?

MAN: Where did you get this milk anyway?

CONVERSATION 4

WOMAN 1: I'm really unhappy about this. I wanted the back a little shorter.
WOMAN 2: Jackie, why didn't you tell him?
WOMAN 1: Well, I tried to, but he didn't really listen. I think he doesn't like customers to tell him what to do.
WOMAN 2: But it's *your* looks and *your money!* I think you should go back and ask him to cut it again.
WOMAN 1: OK. But will you come with me?

Where will the women go?

WOMAN 2: Sure I'll go with you. I know how to talk to hairdressers.

CONVERSATION 5

WOMAN: I want a refund, not an exchange.
MAN: I'm sorry, we don't give refunds without a receipt. It says so right there on the sign.
WOMAN: I know, but how am I supposed to have a receipt if it was a gift?
MAN: Again, I'm really sorry, but that's our store policy. Perhaps we can help you find something else you *really* like, and . . .
WOMAN: Oh, this is really annoying . . .

What will probably happen next?

WOMAN: O.K. I'll just exchange this for some towels.

CONVERSATION 6

WOMAN: Hi. I'm here to pick up my TV set. Here's my receipt.
MAN: Here you are. It's all fixed. It came to $120.
WOMAN: $120!? But it's still under warranty. It's less than two years old.
MAN: You're right. The *parts* are under warranty; so we're not charging you for any parts.

What is the $120 for?

MAN: The $120 is just for labor. The repair work took three hours.

activity 1

It's the end of the school year, and Peter and Kenji are renting an unfurnished apartment for the summer. They are interested in buying a few things, and they are calling people who advertised in the newspaper. Match each telephone conversation with the correct newspaper ad shown on page 119. Circle a, b, or c. As you listen, underline the clues that helped you choose the correct answer.

CONVERSATION 1

A: Hello.

KENJI: Yes, I'm calling about the refrigerator for sale.

A: Uh-huh. What would you like to know?

KENJI: First, how big is it?

A: I'm not sure exactly. . . . It's a normal apartment-sized refrigerator, you know.

KENJI: I see. Does it have a separate freezer?

A: Yes, and it's frost-free.

KENJI: Oh. How old is it?

A: We bought it about four years ago and it was a couple of years old at that time.

KENJI: And it's still working okay?

A: Oh, yeah. It works fine.

KENJI: Can you go any lower on the price?

A: Come on. It's already dirt cheap!

CONVERSATION 2

A: Hello.

PETER: Do you still have your bike for sale?

A: Yes. Which bike were you interested in?

PETER: The Schwinn mountain bike.

A: Oh, yeah, we still have it. It needs new tires, but otherwise it's in perfect shape.

PETER: How much do you want for it?

A: $150. That's half of what I paid for it.

CONVERSATION 3

A: Hello.

KENJI: Hi. I saw an ad in the paper for your TV. Is it still for sale?

A: Well, someone left a deposit on it yesterday, but I'm not sure he's going to buy it. He's going to tell me tonight.

KENJI: Could you tell me a little about it?

A: Yeah. It's a brand new RCA with remote control; the picture's really sharp.

KENJI: Is it under warranty?

A: Sure is. The guarantee covers parts and service for eighteen months.

KENJI: Well, that sounds great. Could you call me tomorrow if the other guy doesn't buy it?

A: Sure. Give me your number.

 A: Hello.

PETER: Hi. Could you tell me a little about the desk you're selling?

 A: Uh, it's a six-foot metal office desk with two filing drawers.

PETER: Can you lock the drawers?

 A: Yeah, but I've lost the key. It's still a really great deal for only $75.

PETER: Okay. I'll come over Saturday to see it then.

activity **2**

Look at the floor plan of the department store. It shows the location of the different departments on the second floor. You will hear people give directions to four departments. Listen to each person and follow the directions. Write the name of each department on the map.

1. Marsha and Mrs. Nutley are at the bottom of the escalator on the first floor. Marsha wants to go to the kitchen department. Mrs. Nutley tells her: "Well, you've got to go up this escalator. Then . . . let me see . . . You'll see the cafeteria on your right. Go around the cafeteria to your right and turn right at the linen department. Then turn left. You'll be in a wide aisle. The linen department is on the left, and the kitchen department is on the right."

2. While she's in the kitchen department, Marsha decides she wants to buy a dress. The salesperson tells her how to find the ladies' dress department. He says to her: "Go out of the kitchen department and turn right around this corner. You'll see a long aisle on your left. Follow that aisle to the end. Turn just before you see the elevators. The dress department will be on your left."

3. While Marsha is paying for the dress, she decides to buy some shoes to go with it. The cashier tells her how to get to the shoe department: "Go out of the dress department and turn right. Make another right and go down to the end of the hall. Turn right at the corner and the shoe department will be on your right."

4. While Marsha is looking at the shoes, she decides to open a charge account with the store. The clerk in the shoe department tells her how to get to the credit department: "Go out of the shoe department and turn left. Turn left again at the corner. Go down to the end of the hall and turn right past the elevators. You'll see the credit department on your right."

Listen to the directions again. Then check your answers with a classmate.